Making Sense of the News

ISBN 0-935742-07-7

Printed in the United States of America

Cover and book design by Billie M. Keirstead
Art production by Joe Tonelli

Quotation on Page ii from *The Education of David Stockman
and Other Americans* by William Greider. Copyright © 1981,
1982 by William Greider. Reprinted by permission of the
publisher, E. P. Dutton, Inc.

Copies of this publication may be ordered at $3.00 each to cover
printing and mailing from Modern Media Institute, 556 Central
Avenue, St. Petersburg, FL 33701

odern *Media* Institute
556 Central Avenue
St. Petersburg, Florida 33701

A Modern Media Institute Ethics Center Seminar

Preface

In late fall 1980, almost immediately after Ronald Reagan's overwhelming election victory, William Greider, an editor at the *Washington Post*, began a series of off-the-record breakfast meetings with David Stockman, who was to become the administration's budget director.

The purpose, as Greider himself later described it: "I would use him and he would use me."

For Greider the payoff would be an opportunity to write a comprehensive account of how the Reagan administration's economic policies developed in the opening year of his presidency, a narrative which would refute "the simple and shallow version of reality that the news created in its daily slices." Stockman established a continuing contact with a major influential newspaper and created the opportunity to explain in detail at a future date his actions and the reasoning which led to them.

The two met 18 times over a nine-month period, usually on Saturday morning for breakfast at the Hay-Adams Hotel, directly across Lafayette Park from the White House. Greider tape-recorded all of the conversations which were conducted as formal interviews, the reporter asking questions, the high government official providing answers. Some of those answers were on-the-record and were published as news stories by the *Post*. Most material, by agreement, was off-the-record pending publication at a mutually agreed upon date.

In August 1981, after the Reagan tax and budget legislation had cleared Congress, Greider began writing a long narrative, laying out in more or less chronological order the inside story of how the whole economic program had been orchestrated. Included were direct quotations from Stockman detailing his doubts about the Reagan economic program and his fears that it would fail.

The 25,000-word article, titled "The Education of David Stockman," was published in the November issue of *Atlantic* magazine, creating a tempest which nearly cost Stockman his job. Immediately, and over a period of weeks and months, the article also focused national attention on a series of ethical questions involving long-standing relationships between reporters and government officials and the responsibility of newspapers to share information with their readers.

Early in 1982, E.P. Dutton re-published the *Atlantic* article in a book which included a lengthy essay by Greider describing his relationship with Stockman and the nature of news coverage in Washington. The essay also raised some troubling questions:

• Why does the press produce a "daily blizzard of startling information" which leaves readers well-fed but undernourished?

• Why does news coverage of government communicate a great deal less than journalists think it does?

• Why does daily news coverage so frequently fail to tell how and why things happen?

• And why were sophisticated readers shocked by David Stockman's candor but unsurprised at what he said?

Greider provides some answers when he speaks in his essay of a coded dialogue among the Washington elite which "may or may not contribute anything of value to the governance of the republic; at the very least it is a closed conversation which only the sophisticated few can follow. Other citizens may be baffled by it, (but) more likely they are bored because it is so opaque."

Greider professed surprise at the furor raised by publication of his *Atlantic* article, contending that all essential information already had been published in the *Washington Post*, the *New York Times* and elsewhere. At the same time, he acknowledged that the narrative format, and its length, gave readers a more understandable account of a complex and confusing series of events extending over almost a year. He also acknowledged that David Stockman's saying within quotation marks that the administration massaged the numbers, adjusted its computer models to achieve salable results, had far more impact than quotations from an unidentified source.

The Greider book, entitled *The Education of David Stockman and Other Americans*, was reviewed for the *Washington Post* by Harold Evans, former editor of the *Times of London* and the *Sunday Times* and a visiting professor at the Modern Media Institute in St. Petersburg, Florida. Evans liked the book and said it was important. He also was impressed by the number of issues it raised which merited further serious consideration.

Evans proposed that he personally moderate a seminar, funded and sponsored by MMI, which would bring together a group of distinguished editors and writers, scholars and people familiar with the news process inside government. And so it was arranged for January 7 and 8, 1983 at the Don CeSar Hotel on St. Petersburg Beach.

In his letter of invitation to participants, Eugene C. Patterson, MMI board chairman and editor and president of the *St. Petersburg Times*, established some parameters for the discussion by declaring that "the press needs to reinvent its definition of news."

He pointed out that Greider, in his essay, suggested that the press tell stories whole instead of "doling them out in thin slices that bend reality and confuse the public while serving veiled purposes of elite insiders in press and government."

Greider, who resigned from the *Post* to join *Rolling Stone* magazine as Washington correspondent, attended to expand on, explain and, in some instances, defend his theses. The full list of participants included former spokesmen for the White House and the State Department, editors and writers, experts in communication and in the science of measuring comprehension, businessmen and teachers.

No firm conclusions were reached and no prescriptions were written. But there was widespread agreement that most readers are not as faithful as writers and editors assume, and that in many instances they are being short-changed by news stories which fail to help them understand what is happening and why.

Will seminars such as this lead to important changes? Probably not. But newspapers today are far better than those of even 20 years ago and change usually begins with serious conversation about important problems.

Donald K. Baldwin
Modern Media Institute

Participants in the seminar were:

Harold Evans, seminar moderator; former editor, *Times of London* and *Sunday Times*; visiting professor, MMI.

William Greider, Washington correspondent, *Rolling Stone*; author, *The Education of David Stockman and Other Americans.*

Dr. James W. Carey, dean, College of Communications, University of Illinois.

W. E. (Ned) Chilton III, editor and president, *Charleston* (West Virginia) *Gazette.*

Gavyn Davis, London financial consultant; British prime minister's economics staff, 1974-1979.

Kermit Lansner, survey research director, Louis Harris and Associates; former editor, *Newsweek.*

Richard Harwood, deputy managing editor, *Washington Post.*

Dr. James David Barber, political scientist and author, Duke University.

Hodding Carter, producer, "The Inside Story," Public Broadcasting Service; former state department spokesman.

Dr. Roy Peter Clark, associate director, Modern Media Institute.

Ray Jenkins, editorial page editor, *Baltimore Evening Sun*; former deputy White House press secretary.

Gerald Lanson, assistant professor of journalism, New York University.

Howell Raines, Washington correspondent, *New York Times.*

Hobart Rowen, economics columnist, *Washington Post.*

Mortimer Zuckerman, president, *Atlantic* and Boston Properties.

Eugene C. Patterson, editor and president, Times Publishing Co., St. Petersburg, Florida.

Dr. John R. Robinson, research psychologist and author, University of Maryland.

Richard Stout, associate professor, American University, Washington, D.C.

Donald K. Baldwin, Modern Media Institute.

Contents

viii

Introduction

"When I first came to Washington in January 1981, I thought there were a lot of very serious problems in coverage of Washington. After 22 months they don't seem quite as serious. I think in two more years I'll feel damn comfortable. So I'm glad to have this chance to talk to you before my lobotomy."

Howell Raines, the *New York Times*

Maybe the people who write the news just haven't been listening to the people who read it.

"I read the dense-packed stories about the budget, and they sort of flowed from one year to the other," says John Donovan, a professor. "The mind reels."

"I'm glad you're confused, John, because I was, too," says Mary Margaret Slazas, a promotional writer.

They were the outside experts, the people who read the news, at a seminar called "Making Sense of the News," and they were talking about the daily news they received on the progress of President Reagan's tax program of 1981—that seemingly revolutionary program of supply-side economics and tax cuts and promises of balanced budgets.

The shortcomings of the daily news reports became painfully clear in December 1981 when *Atlantic* magazine published an article called "The Education of David Stockman." It was written by William Greider, who was then an editor at the *Washington Post,* and it disclosed the confessions of the man in charge of the national budget that he had been intentionally deceiving the American people about the prospects for the Reagan program. The reporters in Washington—even Greider, who was accused of breaking faith with his readers by withholding the information until the tax bill was passed—all said the deception had been reported before. But, as the tiny sample of readers indicated at this seminar, the message was not getting through.

This seminar was supposed to examine why. The participants disagreed about both the malady and the cure, but no one was prepared to pronounce the symptoms imaginary and dismiss the patient. Their discussion should be viewed as only the beginning of a larger discussion about the way reporters and editors report the news, not just about Washington but about state governments and local governments and all the issues that confront their readers.

William Greider, who is now a correspondent for *Rolling Stone* magazine, produced a small book after his *Atlantic* article appeared. He called it *The Education of David Stockman and Other Americans,* and it contained not only the *Atlantic* article but his views about why people were so surprised at what he wrote. The deception of the White House in the selling of its tax program had been in newspapers all along, Greider says, "albeit in the coded language" of Washington insiders. He assumed "that a conscientious newspaper reader who had followed the story of Reagan's economic policy closely might be titillated, shocked, enraged" by what Stockman said "but that most people would not be surprised by the fundamental points he was making, since, in fact, these points had been made in public print prior to the article."

Greider now believes that the reaction to his article reflects a fundamental failing of newspapers. The people whose profession is communication are simply not getting through to their readers. Reporters are handicapped by the rules about "background" and "off-the-record" information, and they are further handicapped by "the conventions of the press, how a story is written and what meets the standard definition of what is news," he says. "While all the stories are there, the coverage communicates a great deal less than the practitioners think it does."

Readers have been trying to tell editors that for years, but it has not sunk in.

Several years ago, a team of researchers set out to learn whether the readers of newspapers were satisfied with what they read. "Editors seem to take it for granted that you know everything they do," one reader replied. "Give us more information to help us understand what it means and why it is important," said another reader. Added a third, "I often prefer to wait to read the entire story in *Time*. Then I can tell what is important and not important."

Those answers were part of a study commissioned by the American Society of Newspaper Editors and published in 1979 by the Yankelovich, Skelly & White research organization. Among the researchers' many conclusions was the conclusion that readers were having to work too hard to extract the important information from their daily newspapers.

Look at Greider's original assumptions about what people knew. The reader who was "conscientious" and followed "closely" would have already known these things. How many people outside commuting range of Washington, D.C. fit that description? How many people find enlightenment in what writing expert Roy Peter Clark calls the dense-pack school of writing, "which attempts to cluster as much information, jargon and statistical confusion into a paragraph as possible"?

Not many, to judge by the reaction to Greider's article. But is that the fault of the reporters or the readers?

"I think the story was being reported rather well," says Hobart Rowen, the economics reporter for the *Washington Post*. "If people weren't understanding it, it's because they weren't reading it, or didn't want to understand it. It was there. It was not there simply in terms of background or in code words or in code language." Pollster Kermit Lansner, a former editor of *Newsweek*, even cites the fluctuations of the polls as evidence that people were indeed following the waning and waxing of the Reagan-Stockman program.

Psychologist John Robinson of the University of Maryland, who is studying people's comprehension of news, says a large percentage of the people do not understand it. He notes that one of the most popular news shows in Great Britain is news for the deaf, which provides the news slowly with captions across the bottom. He also has a warning: "Leaving something between the lines and thinking the reader is going to get it is a very dangerous practice."

Greider, unwilling to lay the blame on readers for their lack of comprehension, believes there is a "real hunger" to know what is going on in government and that the newspapers would have a market for a more nourishing diet of news. He says he hears much more interesting stories around the drinking fountain in the newsroom than he reads in the newspapers, and he believes reporters should find ways to put their drinking fountain news into the newspapers.

Of course, Greider took nine months and 25,000 words to tell his drinking-fountain story about David Stockman. Contributing to the effectiveness of his article were his knowledge of Stockman himself and his perspective of hindsight after the fight was done. He had time to learn of Stockman's pique over the tennis courts built with federal money near the Stockman family farm, a clue to the Stockman economic philosophy. Greider also had time to decipher the coded language and perfect his prose; Roy Peter Clark notes Greider's success at chopping complex information into digestible chunks and mixing it with interesting quotes or anecdotes that hold a reader's interest.

Time and space are luxuries that daily news reporters simply do not have. Clark compares the daily news to the round-by-round descriptions of important prize fights. "He's up. He's down. He's up. He's down. What you miss," says Clark, "is the moral weight of the narrative, the story of the game."

Howell Raines, who covers the White House for the *New York Times,* likewise chafes at the round-by-round reporting. He believes newspaper reporters and their editors "are still captives of the old pre-electronic-age scoop mentality," which leads papers to compete for headlines over trivial events "that to the general public are arcane." He wants newspapers to "be strong enough" to rely on the wire services for daily news.

What Greider did in *The Education of David Stockman* and what he advocates for deliverers of the daily news is the same kind of "explanatory journalism" advocated by *St. Petersburg Times* editor Eugene Patterson. In 1978, when he was president of the American Society of Newspaper Editors, Patterson proposed that newspapers work harder to identify and simplify issues. "I sense a current self-examination in the press, addressing the question of whether throwing rocks at authority is enough, or whether better reporting of issues should be added to our investigative approach," he said.

Patterson's characterization of the issue begged but one conclusion. Still, his proposal, and Greider's, have met the same resistance as the "interpretive reporting" that was advocated a quarter century ago, when the obvious press failure was not deceptive budget-making but the deceptive witch-hunts of Joseph McCarthy. The skeptics are concerned about the very thing that Clark praised in Greider's article, "the moral weight of the narrative."

Gerald Lanson, who teaches journalism at New York University, speaks for the skeptics. He wants to improve reporting but not change its nature. He worries about the press telling "its version of the truth" in news stories. "If we start muddling facts with interpretation, I, as a reader, will feel cheated," he says. "Why should we trust journalists?" No one really believes "pure objectivity" is possible, he says, but it is a valuable guidepost, reminding reporters to let their readers arrive at their own conclusions of truth.

Richard Harwood, deputy managing editor of the *Washington Post*, offers a view of the press that also cautions against oracular truth-saying. Reporters, like other human beings, are incapable of fully comprehending the complex issues and the bloated government of today. They do not often have the routine access Greider had to the inner sanctum of government. "We have been unable to communicate the truth and the deeper realities of these matters because we don't know," he says. Facing these handicaps with neither the time nor the space to explore an issue, reporters become just "skillful hacks faced with responsibilities we are unable to discharge."

"We want to know what is really going on, as if one can know what is really going on," adds Communications Dean James W. Carey of the University of Illinois. But having suggested that reporters quit thinking of themselves as seekers and transmitters of truth, Carey proposes something even more unorthodox than what Greider and Patterson propose. He wants to see more "ferment" in newspaper writing. "I think if there was a more playful, a more conversational approach, it might lead to far more experimentation and different ways of reporting what happened in a given day. It would lead perhaps to the return of different styles of writing, beyond the factual, the flatfooted, and the reportorial."

Hodding Carter III believes the reporting as well as the writing must change. Carter, who hosts the public television show "Inside Story" and formerly was the chief spokesman at the U.S. State Department, says reporters are paying too much attention to how they're being received by their press colleagues and government policymakers and too little attention to the education of the public. He thinks reporters are lazy and rely mostly on background briefings from government press offices. "You are either at our feet or at our throat, and you are to be treated like a dog accordingly," he says. "We throw you the stuff we want to throw you to keep you at our feet."

Political scientist James David Barber of Duke University suggests that the way news is reported gives readers a sense of order that doesn't really exist. "The impression that the fundamental secret about these leaders is their evil intent or their machinations or conspiracy gives way to the secret that's revealed at the moment when Dorothy steps behind the curtain and sees the real Wizard of Oz sweatily pulling the levers," he says. Greider's article demonstrated the confusion about tax policy among the people who were making it.

But Ray Jenkins, a deputy press secretary for President Carter and now editorial page editor of the *Baltimore Evening Sun,* argues that the reporters both perpetuate a myth of order in government but also attempt to puncture the myth. A president is set up for failure, says Jenkins, who seems to favor perpetuation of the myth until some better means is found to maintain faith in the democracy.

Atlantic magazine publisher Mortimer Zuckerman has a similar concern in a different context. He speaks of reporting on the financial instability of banks or even nations and wonders about the responsibilities of the press. How do they convey this when it might become a self-fulfilling prophecy? What does a journalist do?

The "scoop mentality" of which Howell Raines spoke also creates too cozy a relationship with government officials, suggests British government economist Gavyn Davis. "Most scoops in Britain just involve publishing something the public is going to find out anyway in a couple of days," Davis says. "This is entirely without social benefit, but it gives great professional kudos to newsmen who do it. What it means is that they have to play up to the people who are likely to give them scoops. He finds a general bias toward the government's view of issues, which get more attention than views of outsiders.

Howell Raines raises yet another question about the relationship between the press and the government. He repeatedly expresses concern about the "ethical box" Greider got himself into by storing up this treasure trove of facts about the Stockman deception for a magazine article without ever putting it on the front page of the newspaper he worked for, the *Washington Post.* "I'm wondering why the *Post* didn't figure out a way to purge its off-the-record commitment," says Raines.

The broader question is whether reporters and sources alike abuse the "off-the-record" system. Harwood and *Post* editor Benjamin Bradlee have even tried, on two or three occasions, to crack the pervasive use of backgrounders by publishing photographs of the anonymous source. The little revolts produced guffaws and protests, but no results. And this seminar broached no solution to the problem. It is left for another day.

Indeed, all of the issues are left for another day. They have no simple answer, and the people at this seminar might well object if all newspapers chose the same solution to the problems they discussed. Perhaps the problems are intractable. But as W.E. (Ned) Chilton III of the *Charleston Gazette* in West Virginia says, that doesn't end the matter. "I'll accept the notion that the organization of journalism today is such that you cannot ask of it those things that Bill Greider determines ought to be asked of it," Chilton says. "It is the ultimate cop-out to say that if I describe the current reality to you, I can't do more of what has to be done."

Neil Skene
St. Petersburg Times

News as Event and
News as Code

OPENING STATEMENTS BY:

William Greider
Richard Harwood
James Carey
Gerald Lanson

WILLIAM GREIDER: I have a great advantage. For the first time in my adult life I'm no longer employed by a daily newspaper, so I see weaknesses of the press more clearly than before. I assume all of you have read *The Education of David Stockman and Other Americans* so I would start today by stipulating that I was in an anomalous position in writing the Stockman piece because I was both inside and outside.

While dining with David Stockman every Saturday morning, and also being involved in the production of the *Washington Post,* I assumed that my relationship and contacts with Stockman were not really unique, but were pretty much standard practice in Washington. The only unique quality was that ultimately I described our conversations on the record. However, I had lots of evidence—as I suggested in the book—that a good many other reporters and columnists were getting pretty much the same information from David Stockman and, I presumed, from other officials in the executive branch.

My second assumption was that, given the inhibitions and conventions of the press, most or even all of the important points which David Stockman made on the record in my *Atlantic* article had in fact already been made in newspapers, albeit in the coded language of "senior administration official" or "anonymous source at OMB" (Office of Management and Budget). So I assumed, incorrectly, that a conscientious newspaper reader who had followed the story of Reagan's economic policy closely might be titillated, shocked or enraged by Stockman's candid language, by his unfortunate metaphors and by his general brashness, but that most people would not be surprised by his fundamental points since these points already had been made in public print.

Obviously I was mistaken. I've tried to figure out why I was so wrong. I think it involves the way the news media covers government and communicates what it knows. The conclusion is that while all the stories are there, the coverage communicates a great deal less than the practitioners think it does.

Why is that so? Well, I think the code has a lot to do with it. Those of us who are insiders, past and present, know how to read it. Literally, you can pick up any three of the great newspapers and infer all sorts of combat, shifts, and tales of intrigue from stories which are quite opaque to the general reader. Since I left the *Post* I don't know the newsroom gossip so I have to read three newspapers, not quite as everybody else reads them, but not as I used to. It's a great game, trying to figure out what's really going on.

One story that sticks in my memory is a budget briefing in July. The White House put out numbers which were outrageously wrong, and the anonymous briefer, because he wanted to protect his own integrity, said, "I don't believe this. I know it's wrong, but we're going to put it out anyway."

All three newspapers, working under the inhibitions of the ground rules, reported that an anonymous briefer issued this report, but of course he personally didn't believe it. I read these explanations and recognized an old friend in the syntax. It was very easy for me to call a few people and discover that the anonymous briefer was the budget director. Then in the following weeks the CBO (Congressional Budget Office) and other agencies agreed that, "Yes, that's right, these numbers are meaningless."

That's a small example of the commerce that goes on rather regularly. Everybody is inhibited from really putting the knife to what is clearly intentional duplicity.

I think if you read stories right now, when the administration seems still to be in the throes of deciding exactly what it's going to do with its budget, you will see the same sort of daily blasts from this anonymous source or that anonymous source or this high official or occasionally people who put their names on their opinions. It's a bewildering blizzard for readers who are outside the circle of insiders.

It's very hard if you read on Monday that one senior official says this about tax increases and on Wednesday another unnamed senior official says the

opposite and on Friday you read an analytical piece
that says they all agree that deficits are a big problem.

When I get to the question of why that's so or how
one could change it, it gets a good deal more difficult.
Notwithstanding the critics who portray the press in
a vicious adversarial role, there's much more
collaboration than one realizes. I think you have a
whole series of relationships that guide the reflexes
and also inhibit both sides of the relationship. While
both the government and the press benefit from this
symbiosis, they're also prisoners of it. On the whole
it doesn't help very much if you're an outsider reading
the press. At least it doesn't help as much as reporters
think it does.

When I came to the *Post*, Richard Harwood was
national editor and he started a campaign to not play
that game any more. So for some weeks or months
the *Post* refused to go to background briefings and
refused to participate in any of the rather routine
exchanges in which government officials
communicate anonymously through the press.

I confess I didn't appreciate that effort at the time.
I thought it was just Harwood being cranky. It failed
because inevitably reporters and editors want to be
inside. It's hard for me to envision, frankly, how a
newspaper, or even many newspapers, could organize
that kind of a dramatic departure from the way the
game works and make it stick.

I think it would help if reporters and editors forced
themselves to step back and say, "Okay, we're
communicating clearly enough to our lead audience,
those policymakers, politicians and other reporters.
They all know we're doing a wonderful job of covering
this story in all of its complexities, but what is the
story saying to an outsider?"

I think that once a month, on almost any story,
you should sit down and write some sort of an A to
Z narrative or primer that breaks out of the elite
conversation and tries to speak more broadly to the
subject. I think capable reporters ought to be
reporters, which means they ought to say what they
think is really happening, and what they observe is

really happening. I think there is an extraordinary wall between what gets printed in the newspaper or broadcast on television and what those same practitioners will tell you is happening if you ask them at the drinking fountain.

I'm sure a lot of what is said at the drinking fountain is surmise, gossip and malicious innuendo, but a lot of it is right on the money. It cuts through all the bull and says, "Here's what's happening." That's not a bad standard for reporters. Obviously some would misuse it, but it might also get closer to giving a larger picture of reality.

Finally, as I suggested in the book, instead of being preoccupied with what's going to happen next, papers should ask more frequently and more coherently what really did happen. If you look at the Stockman piece, granting the provocative quotes and all the rest of it, the power is that it says, "Looking back over the last 12 months, here's what really happened."

Newspapers do some of that, but not very much. However, if you look at some of the "sensational stories" of the last 10 or 15 years, nearly all of them have been of that nature. Some reporter said, "I'm going to go back over the ground that was news six months, 18 months, even five years ago, and I'm going to report it very thoroughly and tell people what the real history of that period was."

I'll give you one more small example. In 1981, the *Post*, the *Times*, the networks, everybody devoted an extraordinary amount of space and energy to the discussion and debate over the 1982 fiscal budget. By the fall of 1981 everyone was reporting the debate over the 1983 budget. But not until September 1982 did we finally know what that debate was all about. The answer was a $110 billion federal deficit.

Those stories were played inside in the *Washington Post*, the *New York Times*, and of course the *Wall Street Journal.* They were played inside because it was old news. They'd already predicted a deficit of around $110 billion, so when the figure finally came in there was no point in repeating it. They'd already moved on.

That's a moment when you could have said, "All right, now we have the numbers. Let's go back over that last fiscal year and reconstruct what happened." You remember that the original deficit prediction was $40 billion. When I wrote the *Atlantic* piece, thinking I was out on a limb, I raised it to $60 billion, and that took people's breath away. A year later it's at $110 billion. This still would be a good story if someone went back and without any ideological or partisan economic theories at work simply told people, "Here's how it got from $40 billion to $110 billion."

I would finish by putting this in a larger context because I really think there is a larger argument over what news is, what newspapers think they're doing, and what they are responsible for.

This is the most subversive thought I have, and I owe it to Dr. James David Barber. I was attending a seminar at Duke and all these professors were sitting around rapping the press. They asked in effect, "Are the news media responsible to their audience? Are they responsible for what their audience knows and understands?" A dozen reporters and TV types were at the table, and all of us unanimously said, "Hell no, that's not what we do. We do news."

It took me a good long while to understand, first of all, what was implied in that question. It also took some time to switch sides and to say that, yes, in the 1980s the news media must have some level of responsibility for what people know and understand. I think that's a crucial question.

Let me just read the one sentence from Walter Lippmann which I remember reading years ago and rebelling against. Lippmann said, "The function of news is to signalize an event. The function of truth is to bring to light the hidden facts, to set them into relation with each other, and to make a picture of reality on which men can act."

Lippmann had a very elitist view of how American democracy was supposed to work. He said newspapers were not supposed to mess around with meaning and truth and all those big things. They were merely to tell what happened and most of that they were going to get wrong. A lot has changed since Lippmann wrote that, but I think that split is still very much in the ethos of news coverage.

Everybody recognizes that the complexity of public life and modern events doesn't permit a stenographic approach to news any more. Every reporter really does make a series of judgments. Every editor makes judgments behind those, which are their own definitions of meaning, even if they deny that they're searching for meaning.

Among my models for the way I think newspapers ought to do lots of things are the best European newspapers, including the *Sunday Times* of London. They assume a much broader charter of what it is they're doing. But there's a big difference between those newspapers and American newspapers in terms of audience. The best newspapers in Europe are elitist. They speak only to a very narrow band of the population. They make no attempt to speak to everyone. They presume that the rest of the population probably wouldn't understand anyway.

An American editor or publisher starts with a very different premise, which is that his audience is the whole spectrum of society, regardless of education, income and everything else. While there's always some hypocrisy in that, it's the premise of metropolitan newspapers in America, and I think it's right.

The only point I would add is that in the realm of economics, but in other areas as well, we have a really bizarre situation. Educational levels are higher than ever, information levels are more streamlined and modernized and thorough, and yet the electorate is increasingly alienated and disaffected from the processes of democracy.

On an even more serious level we have watched in the last 10 or 15 years the political cycle playing out its set of promises and the economic cycle in our country and the world playing out a different time cycle. The media is one of the few connecting points between those two cycles, and only the media can attack the mythology that one controls the other or that everything is as neat and rosy as the politicians tell us it is. If the media doesn't do that, then I think we're all prisoners in this country.

HAROLD EVANS: Bill made a lot of good points and I made some notes on a few of them. One is that we should get back to the description of what's really going on. Too much journalism is stenography, and not enough journalism is the first draft of history. Those are some of the prescriptive things that might emerge, but underlying that he's made a basic analytical point, and I'm going to ask Dick Harwood to reply.

He said, first of all, that he wrote nothing new in the *Atlantic* article and anybody who reads the code could have found it in the daily papers. Secondly, he said there was very little public understanding of what was being said opaquely in the press.

I'd like for all of us to concentrate, if we can, on this basic point before we turn to what might be done about it and whether the press is responsible for imposing a false sense of efficiency and order on an otherwise chaotic series of news events.

Now, could I ask Dick Harwood to reply for the press to the Greider thesis.

RICHARD HARWOOD: Let me put on my reporter's hat. I've been assigned to cover this speech. I'm on deadline and I've been given three inches. I think I wouldn't even use three inches. I'd take one sentence to sum up what he's saying—that when a newspaper comes out every day an unsatisfactory transaction occurs. Something doesn't get communicated, and I agree with that. But I want to approach it from a somewhat different perspective.

At one point in his essay Bill refers to his "unique arrangement" with David Stockman. He also describes it as a "fairly routine arrangement." The distinction is important to this discussion because it gets to the question of what journalists know about "truth" and "deeper realities." It gets to the question of when they know it. And those things in turn get to the question of why we in journalism communicate in such imperfect and unsatisfactory ways.

If the central problem is, as Bill suggests, the inhibiting conventions of journalism and politics, then a remedy is in sight. We need only invent new conventions or operating rules. If the central problem is something else, as I will argue, then a different remedy is required.

I begin with notions of romance and mythology that may be psychologically essential to the enterprise of journalism but which are not useful in defining who we really are and what we really do. The first of these notions is that of the journalist as an "insider" operating, in Bill's phrase, in a "netherworld of continuous private conversations" that enable reporters and columnists to know "how government officials really feel." This Lanny Budd image of the reporter is enhanced by such memoirs as Ben Bradlee's "Conversations With Kennedy" and Cy Sulzberger's autobiography. We find them fascinating and revealing precisely because insider relationships of that nature are exceptional.

I sometimes wish that we were all Lanny Budds, consorting with kings, prime ministers and leaders of the free world. But that is not the way the world of journalism really works. In the main, we are outsiders, collecting little scraps of information here and there to make puzzle solutions in our heads. Our access to and relationships with those we ought to know—and with the great men and women of government as well—are often accidental, shallow and marred by mutual suspicions. The adversarial atmosphere is strong and it does not contribute to intimate or confessional relationships in which "truthtelling," as Bill uses the word, is a common transaction. What really went on in the discussions that led the joint chiefs of staff to vote three to two against the dense-pack plan for the MX missile? What is really being said within the Treasury Department about the international banking system? What is the CIA really saying about operations in Central America? What is really going on between the United States and Angola? We have been unable to communicate the truth and the deeper realities of these matters because we don't know. The necessary political-journalistic relationships either do not exist or we have been unable to use and exploit them. We confront that reality every day—the reality of not knowing, the reality of non-access. Thus, our frequent problem is not the corruption that may arise out of too close dealings and the private sharing of secrets. It is rather the problem of being too distant from those whose personalities, beliefs, knowledge, hopes and fears are essential to the understanding we would communicate to our countrymen.

One of the causes of this difficulty is simply scale. The governmental and economic universe with which we deal has grown almost beyond our comprehension. The number of people carrying press cards has grown apace. In some ways this growth has been beneficial to the citizen in terms of information he needs. Specialized journals, newsletters and newspaper articles are frequently impressive. But bloated institutions also have made the task of the journalist more difficult. Knowledge, information and the decision-making processes themselves have become fragmented beyond the ability of many of us to absorb. So the scale of things helps create the lonely crowds I have described—actors and critics dealing with one another in formalized, fleeting and impersonal ways.

A compensation for this condition has been a growing reliance in Washington on exile or alternative governments—the lobbies, the think tanks and congressional subcommittees. They are often helpful. But they are not a solution to the problems Bill recites.

In attempting to define a more useful and more relevant style of journalism, Bill proposes to modify the conventions of our trade to allow the reporter to "tread beyond the safe limits of what is knowable from daily reporting into the analytical realm where the reporter is obligated to make sense of things for the reader. The best new journalism will take the risks and try to go deeper—not self-indulgently or for partisan advantage—but to share with the reader or TV viewer what the reporters themselves understand to be happening." This is a sensible notion. It is compatible with the conventions we now observe. Discovering and writing the meaning of things has, in fact, become one of the abiding commandments. If that is true, why then do we continue to produce the "daily blizzard of startling information" that leaves the reader well-fed but undernourished?

One obvious answer is the nature of the business. So long as we publish 365 days a year, so long as we produce our prose within an hour or two, so long as we have deadlines and expanses of white space to fill, so long as we are purveyors of news, the blizzards will continue and Bradlee's familiar phrase will remain true: "a first rough draft of history." A second and contentious answer is that newspapers are approximately as good as they can be on any given day. I mean that we produce a product that rather accurately reflects the level of our professional and intellectual capacities. We are not efficient in communicating truth and deeper reality because of restrictive conventions or inhibiting rules. The deficiency is in us as human beings and as communicators. Bill Greider for a time wrote a biweekly essay under the title, "Against the Grain." It was superb and it died with his departure from the *Post.* Like Lazarus, it could rise again tomorrow were it not for one problem: No one has come forth with the capacity to do it.

We will come closer to Bill's ideal newspaper when better thinkers, better writers and better reporters come along. But we should not delude ourselves now about our capabilities. Most of us in the news business today are not as profound or as wise as we would wish or as we may be perceived. If you will watch a few weeks of the Martin Agronsky show you will appreciate what I mean. We work, ordinarily, near the limits of our capabilities. But in many cases we are, as the mass of newspaper people always have been, skillful hacks faced with responsibilities we are unable to discharge.

EVANS: I think before I turn to the people I have on the program, James Carey and Gerald Lanson, I would like to invite some of the press people to respond. Bill Greider said there's no understanding and Dick Harwood said, yes, there is no understanding, and we can't give it.

Do you accept that criticism, Ned?

W. E. (NED) CHILTON: I accept a lot of it. I'm wondering about one thing that Bill said earlier with respect to the symbiosis between government and the press—the *Post,* the *Times,* papers like that. The rural press doesn't have such relationships. I'm wondering if that symbiosis would be broken if the papers would play hard ball, putting a reporter in the Pentagon for two years, then transferring him out.

HOWELL RAINES: I want to make a point that relates to the background process, one of the things Bill's talking about.

If you are the political editor of the *St. Petersburg Times,* as I've been, or if you are the editorial page editor of the *Montgomery Advertiser,* as Ray Jenkins has been, you can muscle into being in your state a set of rules destructive of the background system. You can say, "Talk to us on the record, or we won't play." The multiplicity of media in Washington makes this impossible.

HODDING CARTER: I suggest that that's nonsense. In fact, a handful of players could dominate the system if they chose to do so. You suggested that to the newsmaker this vast number of outlets matters. So few matter, that if a small handful decided the game should be played a different way, it would be played a different way. And Dick (Harwood), I wish you would speak to why that experiment failed.

HARWOOD: Different people have different explanations. Bradlee's explanation is that if three or four papers had gone along, it would have worked. These would have to have included the *New York*

Times, the *Wall Street Journal* and maybe, at that time, the *Star.* These and the news magazines and the networks wouldn't play. That's one explanation. The other is that I don't think there was any tremendous internal drive on the part of reporters because it's easy. One of the reasons they love the system is that they don't have very much access. How do I get to see the secretary of state? Well, I go to his backgrounder, and dine out on that for a few weeks.

I think that if you did gang up you could change a lot of those things. At the same time, you've got behavior modification problems with your own editors and reporters that are awfully hard to break.

RAINES: I want to respond to Hodding. I think his criticism of my point proves it, because he is saying that a level of coordination is necessary to break this system. I think that proves my point that the game is so diverse and so broad that a single institution, or even a group of institutions, couldn't dominate and control it.

I want to respond to Dick Harwood on this point. He is implying that reporters perpetuate the background tradition. I would suggest that editors perpetuate it. I have heard any number of high-minded discourses about taking information on background: "Let's don't do it if it's serving their ends rather than ours."

As a beat reporter on the *New York Times* or the *Washington Post,* if you refuse background information and the next morning your competitor has a story quoting an anonymous source and you have been beaten, your editors do not have the backbone to take the heat. You, as the reporter, and your superior as a news editor, will be caught in the middle of a serious manure storm the morning after you've been beaten.

HOBART ROWEN: I think that's absolutely true. I think you're both right. Reporters do find it easy to accept what's given at backgrounders, but the heat and the pressure come from the competitive situation.

If you're on the *Washington Post* you don't want to pick up the *New York Times* and find a basically sound budget deficit story from a backgrounder if you haven't got it.

EVANS: That proves the point that you are playing the game of the government.

ROWEN: No, that wasn't the point I was trying to make. I was trying to agree with Howell. It's the competitive situation that perpetuates the backgrounder.

RAY JENKINS: Let's not forget the usefulness of the backgrounder as an institution. Maybe we're just assuming that it's a bad thing, that honesty requires that we tell who is saying what.

I don't think that's true at all. Communication is made up of levels that are very identifiable in Washington—backgrounder, off the record, for guidance only, on the record, this, that, and the other. These have been developed over a long time.

In a background session it's government speaking, or an administration or an institution. If you give it a face or a name it distracts from the issue being discussed or the information being imparted. It becomes not the government's information, but that of an individual—Haig or Shultz or some third rank bureaucrat.

Let's don't automatically assume that the backgrounder, or this form of communication, is dishonest. It may be more honest than the other way.

EUGENE PATTERSON: When you and Jody Powell were running the Carter White House press office, if the Harwood rule had been in effect, would you simply have given no background information? Would you have gone to ground and kept it a secret?

JENKINS: I don't think that's necessarily true. Most background information is not given out as a leak. That's an altogether different form of communication, but nonetheless a part of it. I think it would have been much harder.

During the Iran situation, when Hodding Carter became as familiar on the nightly news as John Chancellor, I think viewers wondered whether this was the United States government speaking or was Hodding Carter up there making policy? I think the reader may have been a little confused.

PATTERSON: Getting away from Iran, Hodding, in your general job at the State Department would ending the background briefings have stopped the flow of information?

CARTER: Stopping the backgrounder initially would obviously deprive folks of some information. But I'm all in favor of doing away with the backgrounder because most backgrounders are not an attempt to do the faceless job of government, but to do the faceless job of a particular faction within government, confusing the public a great deal because it's not allowed to identify the faceless faction or to reveal from whence cometh this information. It is blindsiding, and it's the people who really get blindsided.

The fact is, all arrangements we have are a conspiracy among major organizations. The elaborate rules of a backgrounder are a conspiracy which any one of you can break any time you want to by violating the difference between deep background and background and off the record. This has all been elaborately worked out among news organizations. In anything except the short run the backgrounder is a bad deal for the public. It's a great deal for the press and for the government office.

GREIDER: Go a step further. Suppose these news organizations all agree to go to some higher level? What happens six months later?

CARTER: It's like classification. You know, 90 percent of all the classified stuff I ever saw could have been released without a bit of damage to anybody, including the personalities involved.

One reason for backgrounding is the same as the reason for classification—the control of information. It's power, and your ability to manipulate that power is central to your ability to get ahead in Washington. This is true for the press as well as it is for the government.

GREIDER: But Dick Harwood's point is that the reporters, with rare exceptions, really don't have access to the inside of that factional fight. Do you think the press would be able to report those factional disputes without the background?

CARTER: Yes, because the disputes are usually of a basic enough nature that the people involved are going to get to you because they are fighting about things they really care about.

The other part of it is that within every beat most reporters I know are involved very much in an insider's game in which the amount of material they know but don't use at least equals the amount of material they do use.

CHILTON: I want to ask you a question. If you're talking on television, that's one thing. But if you're doing a backgrounder and the press is there and the public doesn't understand that backgrounder, aren't we failing to give our readers full information?

CARTER: If you're going to live in this world, the very least that ought to be done is to identify precisely the angle from which the material comes, what kind of viewpoint is being expressed.

JENKINS: Can't the press, though, identify the institution which is speaking as opposed to the individual?

CARTER: Yes, but on the Stockman story the running problem was that you may have known it was

Stockman, and a lot of inside boys may have known it was Stockman. I didn't know who that guy was, and frankly it would have altered my whole interpretation of what was going on if I had at least been told that it was an OMB type saying these figures were nonsense.

EVANS: Could I ask those who were reporting the Stockman story whether you went along and talked to people and peddled faction stories? That's one question. The second question is, if you had refused to do that, had not attended the background briefings, would you have been able to give the public more understanding of what was going on, and did you know what was going on?

Was Dick Harwood right in saying that you didn't know what was going on? Bill Greider's thesis this morning was that it was all being published.

ROWEN: I don't think Dick is right about that, and I'm surprised to hear Hodding say that he didn't know about Stockman. I think the story was being reported rather well. When I say "the story," I mean the essential contradiction of the Reaganomics philosophy, the idea that you could pump $700 billion worth of tax cuts into the economy, raise the defense budget, have a tight monetary policy and make it all come out with 4 percent real growth and a balanced budget in 1984.

From the very beginning of the presentation of that budget, not from background briefings with Stockman or anybody else, but from analytical studies of economists, government officials, private officials, and our own brains, we were able to put together a perfectly good, reasonable, continuing story. For a long, continuous period we analyzed the story and told it well. If people weren't understanding it, it's because they weren't reading it, or didn't want to understand it. It was there. It was not there simply in terms of background or in code words or in code language.

That's the part of Bill's book that bothers me most, the suggestion that somehow we have all descended into some new symbiotic relationship where we talk in code only to the elite. I reject that.

PATTERSON: We were saying editorially in the *St. Petersburg Times* before the election that Reaganomics didn't make sense. Isn't there a distinction here between commentary, editorial comment, analysis and reporting in the Greider sense?

ROWEN: I don't think there's much difference. One of the theses presented here is that we should narrow the distinction between facts and interpretation. Bill (Greider) suggested this morning that we ought to pattern ourselves more after the British press. I don't agree, but that's a separate issue.

What we were saying during the campaign was different from what we were able to say once that budget and that economic forecast were produced. It obviously contained a self-destruct mechanism, and the press said so. That story was written in our paper, the *New York Times, Business Week*, in *Newsweek*, in *Time* magazine.

What Bill did was something unique. It was a tremendous contribution to journalism that he not only pulled it all together, but he did it in words and quotes from David Stockman which showed that the analysis of outsiders was correct, and this same analysis was being made at a high level within the administration. This cast a great deal of doubt on the essential character of David Stockman. It was a tremendous piece of journalism.

My problem with Bill is not the education of David Stockman. My problem is with some of the conclusions he comes to in the surrounding essays. I don't believe he's illustrated any tremendous weakness in the press. I think we have, on different levels for different audiences, conveyed a great deal of the story in context and in depth.

MORTIMER ZUCKERMAN: I had a different reaction to the *Atlantic* piece than the whole issue of Reaganomics. My reaction was that it was really telling the story in personal terms. Somebody was saying publicly for the first time, contrary to his whole image, "We didn't know what was going on. We didn't know what the numbers were. We only had three or four weeks or six weeks to put these numbers together. We just threw them together. We knew it wasn't going to work. The thing was put together so fast. It should have been put together differently." If you suddenly translate supply-side economics and trickle-down theories into a tax cut for the rich, you undermine a lot.

That seems to me to be something entirely new. When you put it all together in personal terms, when somebody actually cooking the dinner comes out of the kitchen and says, "Hey guys, we didn't put soup in here. It's all water," you have a totally different sense of what was going on within the administration.

Somebody could at least have argued that if you cut certain kinds of taxes there would be a surge in investments, et cetera, but what became clear, it seems to me, was that nobody believed that.

David Stockman, the whiz kid with his new program, all the analysis at his fingertips, all the facts at his fingertips, didn't have the analysis, he didn't have the facts, he didn't have the belief, and he was saying this publicly.

GREIDER: Just as a followup, let me read you two quick sentences, because I'm arguing only that that wasn't news. The fact that Stockman had said it in quotes was news.

"The predictions for inflation growth, business investment, and unemployment, and so on, are mostly guesswork. The Reagan team can accurately say that forecasts by their Keynesian predecessors didn't work out well, but only a hope and a prayer lay behind their own 'off-the-wall' data, a curious emphasis of contradictory supply-side and monetary things. Privately, officials admit that when they don't like one set of numbers, they introduce new assumptions until they get numbers they like better."

CARTER: It was not useful for those who were theologically, philosophically, politically opposed to the Reagan philosophy before the fact to have been writing about the budget. The audience out there saw the *St. Petersburg Times,* saw you, saw me, as discredited by having opposed the guy they had just given a mandate to. The question is not whether those who were exponents of a certain economic philosophy were defeated at the polls for saying this thing wouldn't work. The question is, what was the larger press doing about describing the government as composed of folks going about a rational business in a rational way, doing things as part of some master plan.

Based on the stories I read, I would defy anybody to identify David Stockman, unless they were insiders.

RAINES: I think we're dancing around an ethical question posed by all this. The job of a reporter and a newspaper is to bring, as Hodding said, information to the public.

Every time you take off-the-record information, therefore, you create a potential ethical dilemma for yourself. At some point you're going to find out something the public ought to know and yet, as an honorable person, you may be bound by ground rules that prevent your telling it. This story becomes dramatic when we find out that the cook is fixing the soup, when we get the cook acknowledging that it's water—in this case, when Stockman says to Greider, "I am fixing the numbers." At that point, it seems to me, the *Post* is in a terrible dilemma. It's not common practice, you know. Here we've got the man himself saying, "I am fixing this. I'm cooking these numbers."

At that point, isn't the *Post* compromised by not being able to tell its readers bluntly and directly, "Okay, here's what's happening. The architect of Reaganomics is cooking the numbers"?

EVANS: Did Stockman say that to you too?

ROWEN: I think in this case it was not Stockman.

EVANS: Let me put you on the spot. Could you have broken your promise and scooped Greider by saying, "Stockman doesn't believe his figures?" Is it an unfair question?

GREIDER: That story was written. In fact Bart (Rowen) wrote it and I think John Barry also wrote it. Stockman and others were rearranging the computer model of what would happen in the economy to suit their own theories.

ROWEN: This was written in late January or early February. At that point Stockman did not say they were cooking the numbers to lie. He just said, "We're changing the model." That's one of the things that really outraged a number of people. In terms of the ethical conflict, yes, absolutely, but that is not a unique situation. Every reporter who enters into those arrangements has the same ethical dilemma.

GAVYN DAVIS: The two questions I'd like to ask William (Greider) are: First, why does he think people crave understanding? People don't crave understanding. They probably are getting all they want. The papers are businesses. They're selling a product. Maybe they know better than William does what people will read.

Second, why does he think people want old news? Why should people be interested in the 1981-82 budget? As a financial market participant, I'm interested in what I have to fund this year. I'm not interested in why I had to fund it last year. So while I agree with your basic thesis, there are massive problems.

GREIDER: As an American who believes in the almost mystical "small-d" democracy, I have to believe that people want to understand what it is they're engaged in. Beyond mysticism, I think my own experience tells me that is true. I concede that there will always be a market for easy answers, maybe even a majority market, and that there will always be a market, and a profitable one, for frivolity and craziness.

At the same time, again from my personal experience, I find repeatedly in talking to people much more sophistication and earnestness than I was giving them credit for. There is a real hunger, expressed in very direct terms, to know what is going on. People say to reporters, editors, government officials, "I can't make any sense out of all this."

I think it goes a great deal further than that. I think the media underestimates its audience and that if it concentrated on translating from those writers for elite audiences to a broader audience a market would be there.

CARTER: The notion that these larger and more complex questions cannot be transmitted to a larger audience because they are confusing to the practitioners flies in the face of a great deal of what we understand about public participation over the last decade.

As one who used to have to go out and argue the case for certain administration policies, it was a usual experience to discover in every community people who were well informed and opposed to our policy on SALT.

Today, one of the nice things about the nuclear freeze movement is that the high priests of the mythology of security analysis find that they are arguing with people who at least are able to argue them to a draw. Why? Because the material is made increasingly available outside the priesthood. One of the problems about the way the press operates, in issue after issue, is that it accepts the assumptions of the priests and refuses to try to demythologize for a larger audience.

JOHN ROBINSON: Why do you (Greider) want newspapers to do fundamentally the job that magazines are doing? And in fact, your article appeared in a magazine and then moved into the press later. So is this really a new function you're describing for newspapers?

The other question I have is, why was Stockman able to get away with what he did? We are supposed to have a system of checks and balances. Where was Congress? Where were the other people checking him? Why was he able to get away with what he was able to get away with?

An economist who left the Reagan administration was quoted the other day as saying, "The problem we had in the first year was that we put together a ridiculous budget and we got everything we asked for."

EVANS: I'm going to ask Jim Carey, who's with the University of Illinois, to lead off with a response to both the Stockman explosion in the papers and to what we've said this morning.

JAMES CAREY: Let me try to pick through notes made while listening to everyone this morning and reading over the advance readings. My comments will be not as an outsider, but as someone who is a reasonably faithful reader of the daily newspaper, and who's not an "insider" in any sense of the word.

In a general way, at least, I agree with the analysis that Bill Greider has provided. I don't know how people, even by faithful reading of the newspaper, get a particularly good sense of what's going on. It certainly requires an enormous amount of work, unless of course one brings to it a substantial theoretical knowledge of the fields involved.

Most people do not have either such a theoretical knowledge or the ideological filters to judge economic matters. This makes it very hard, because the newspaper itself does not provide its own context of interpretation. It presents information, and information is often disconnected, not merely in historical time, but in terms of the relationship of items to one another.

There is in Bill's essay a kind of paradox because we have built this enormous apparatus, this periodical system which churns out information on a daily, weekly and monthly basis. We're awash in information. Yet at the same time there is less understanding and more difficulty in gaining that understanding. Information seems to move faster than ever before, but I have the idea that ideas move more slowly, that they perhaps never have moved more slowly.

Walter Lippmann pointed out that the press cannot substitute for other social institutions that cultivate theoretical knowledge, ideological positions, and some kind of comprehensive capacity. But I think also that often many of the techniques and conventions of the press don't help us a great deal in trying to gain this understanding. Often when I encounter journalists after hours in strange situations I seem to get a better rendering of what is going on than I got from reading it. I'm always fascinated by what was not in the paper that they're quite willing to tell me, and it doesn't strike me as libelous or slanderous. I usually walk away with some sense of, "By God, that's really interesting. I think I understand something a little better now."

I think that the techniques of daily news reporting provide a much more coherent sense of what the world is than it actually is. It's more ordered, it's more put together, it's more rational. People seem to know what they are doing. Yet most of us do not believe this. Even when we work in smaller institutions, we know how disordered they are, how badly they're functioning. The budget information of my own university is about like the budget information from the federal government. No one grasps it. There's a new set of numbers every day. They change all the propositions which generate the data, but based on your experience with other institutions you can make the necessary corrections. When you finish reading the news accounts, however, you sense that the world is better structured and more orderly than it truly is.

In addition, there is a tendency to focus too much on personality and motive, to focus on the man and not on the ideology. Often I expect I'm reacting because I'm much more interested in people's positions on issues than in what they're like as individuals, what their motives are or what their character is.

EVANS: You wouldn't accept, then, that personalities help to enliven and dramatize what is being said in code? Is that what you're saying?

CAREY: Well, it may enliven and dramatize, but I think that all too often it is overdone.

It seems to me that journalism operates on the assumption of the constant reader. This is the reader who queues up every day and does his civic duty, putting his money down and putting in a couple of hours finding out what's going on. The whole system turns upon that person being there, because the journalist can't write as if people come in and out of the audience randomly and read randomly. They have to make some assumptions about what people know, what they read yesterday. They have to assume some kind of continuous process of self-education and insight into the political process.

Many of these things become even more pronounced when you turn to economics, the dark continent of journalism. The newspaper was established as an instrument for the merchant and trader. They needed to know every morning what were the prices, what was available to be bought and sold. When the economic trader reads that IBM is at 65, he knows whether that is a good number or a bad number and what he is supposed to do about it. So it started as a business press and then spread to reporting all sorts of other things which don't cycle down to this businessman quite the same way.

I wonder whether journalism does or can or even should get at what's really going on. It doesn't reveal what is really going on, we argue on one side, because conventions don't allow it, nor do the time pressures under which the press must operate. Journalists are looking for what Dewey called "a neurotic quest for certainty." Another philosopher called it "the desire for metaphysical comfort." We want to know what is really going on, as if one can know what is really going on. I wonder if some problems of journalism would be eased if journalists had a different self-understanding of what they are doing, one that does not make them seekers of truth, revealers of reality. Instead, what if they tried to produce a newspaper of record that preserves most of what is important during a given day. This is a very important record for all of us because a lot of history, social science and literature are written from it.

EVANS: Isn't that what journalists are doing now, though?

CAREY: I think they're trying to say something else. Their relationship to me is one of transmitting some truth, however degenerate, of trying to inform me, of making me better informed.

I think that a more modest and more conversational concept of what is going on would be useful. When I speak of a more conversational concept I mean that journalists might feel free to produce more frivolous things, more playful things, and to engage in some different kinds of writing. You may not agree with me, but one of the things I'm struck by is the great ferment going on currently in American writing. There's a melding of intellectual disciplines. As one person put it, pretty soon we're going to see quantum physics in verse and biography in algebra.

You can't quite figure out what some of the things being produced are. They're not quite fact, they're not quite fiction. Philosophy increasingly looks like a political tract. Yet at the same time I don't see this kind of ferment in journalistic writing. There is not the same kind of experimentation, the same attempt by the daily newspaper to do things differently. I think if there was a more playful, a more conversational approach, it might lead to far more experimentation and different ways of reporting what happened in a given day. It could lead to the return of different styles of writing, beyond the factual, the flatfooted, and the reportorial.

I would like to see a more partisan, ideological press, frankly and openly arguing with me on a daily basis. I'm quite confident of my own ability and the ability of others to accept, to reject, to tell you you're crazy for taking such a position.

I think that if journalists did not feel a responsibility to produce some version of reality, but would become an important partner in a conversation about our own culture, there would be many different tones of voice, many more political voices, a wider variety of commentary. I suppose I'd let the facts take care of themselves.

PATTERSON: I hear Jim Carey saying that he's tired of the press as preacher, that he wants us to be a little less elevated and a little more conversational, even frivolous, more partisan, arguing with him instead of telling him what the truth is, questions and answers instead of answers only.

Earlier he said something that causes me to ask, what is the role of the press in a self-governing society? Is it simply this frivolous vehicle that Carey described, or did he come closer to putting a serious question to us earlier when he said press accounts are more coherent than the actual world? The reader gets a sense that the world is better structured and ordered than it really is from our accounts, which of course echoes Hodding Carter's earlier comment that we need to demythologize the government because the press is imposing a false sense of order on chaotic government processes.

What is our responsibility with regard to Lippmann's picture of reality on which reasonable people can act, and at what point in covering the government do we destroy the institution that we're free to serve or attack?

The British military scholar, John Keegan, wrote a superb book called *The Face of Battle* in which, as a military history professor at Sandhurst, he studied why military science is taught as it is to the officer cadres of the Western armies. Every man is drilled and drilled and drilled so he will respond to that conditioning under the blast and the explosion and the blood and the chaos of the battlefield. But he is not taught about the blast and the explosion and the blood and the chaos. He is not taught that because it's unacceptable.

This comes back to my question. What is the balance? What does the press owe the government of this society in being hostile to its institutions and taking no responsibility for being more than a frivolous or conversational arguer in creating pictures on which reasonable men can act? Or do we have some responsibility toward making order out of the admitted chaos of our government and even our press processes?

GREIDER: I don't have millenial views about the ability of anybody to tell the truth or to know the truth. I don't think that's given to human nature. And I agree that if the expectations of people toward their daily newspaper or television were altered to be less prophetic, then that would in fact breed reporters who would write in different voices and would be not only more interesting and entertaining, but would probably be somehow closer to the truth and what they really felt, knew or thought.

One of the problems is that you're really talking about the economic organization of the mass media, and what you (Carey) are describing existed 80 or 100 years ago. I don't think we're going to go back to that. That multiplicity of voices served much narrower audiences, and therefore could speak through their own ideological, partisan, religious, ethnic screens in a way familiar to each particular audience.

CAREY: Are you saying that you don't think that kind of a marketplace of ideas would sell?

GREIDER: No, all I'm trying to describe is the dilemma of a mass circulation newspaper. It has collected all these different audiences under one tent, and it knows that. It may not articulate it, but it knows that there are different groups out there, and as a result it has homogenized its voice over the years into something called "objectivity." Indeed, it has created this pretense that, "Hey, we're just giving you the facts, and it's the straight unbiased truth," when all of the practitioners know that cannot be done.

JAMES DAVID BARBER: I think that *The Education of David Stockman* is making a much more profound point than has generally been appreciated here. The number one secret is chaos rather than conspiracy. We might have been misled during the Nixon-Johnson period into thinking that what we had to worry about was Talleyrand in the Oval Office, when really what we had to worry about was Warren Harding. That is the secret of a great many institutions in American life, including the press, but also the government and the world. The impression that the fundamental secret about these leaders is their evil intent or their machinations or conspiracy gives way to the secret that's revealed at the moment Dorothy steps behind the curtain and sees the real Wizard of Oz sweatily pulling the levers.

There's a story there. It seems to me to be a revealable story, and Bill suggested a way of handling it, by contemplating the difference between anticipation stories and retrospective stories. I'm very aware as a student of political biography that before a president takes power we have a completely different image of him or his successor than retrospectively.

I think the second secret he brings out—and this is the burden of Bill's book, as distinct from the revelations in the article—is that we know very little about our consumers. That's true not only of the press, but of the law, of medicine, of the academic world. We all are operating under an enormous burden of ignorance about the effect of medicine on patients, of the legal process on clients, of the academic world on students.

Certainly that's true about the press. Most of what we are talking about here is sheer speculation about how you're being received, even by Constant Reader, and the best estimate you can probably make is that you're not being received very much by anyone.

Still another secret is more frightening than chaos. We may be in a period in which we don't really care very much about the facts. One sees that in the reporting of facts about Mr. Reagan. Just a few years ago when a president made a mistake, the press was all over him. It analyzed Jimmy Carter's lust in the heart and Gerald Ford's Polish liberation, and now this guy Reagan gets away with murder. I think that points to an enormous social problem. Ever since Troy we've known that you can greatly overestimate the attraction of reality and underestimate the attraction of illusion to people. Certainly the history of Marxism is a prime example of the victory of illusion.

The point is that fiction is neat, life is ragged. Fiction is engaging, life is frustrating. It worries me that so much of the discourse now really doesn't seem to give a damn. This relates to the "Jimmy's World" story in the *Washington Post*. A lot of people were saying, "Well, maybe that wasn't true, but surely there's bound to be an eight-year-old addict somewhere, and so it's a sort of truth."

David Gergen, our president's PR man says, "Well, our president now, he talks in parables."

HARWOOD: This discussion, I think perpetuates a little mythology in that it focuses on a perception of the press as the Fourth Estate, a participant in governing, in the democratic process. Indeed we do some of that, but I started thinking about what we do. What does the *Washington Post* do every day?

In our news department we have roughly 525 people, of whom fewer than 20 percent are engaged in what you might call Fourth Estate business. About 75, including people who answer telephones, are involved in national or international reporting. So this leaves, let's say, 400 people doing something else, and what do they do? Well, they produce the home section; they produce the style section; they produce the sports section; they produce the financial section. We devote more space every day to comics than we devote to national news. I raise this point to again get to the mythology of what newspapers do.

CHILTON: Your description of reality is fine, and you described it well, except you didn't take the percentages far enough. When you eliminate the editorial page, the opposite editorial page, the comic pages, the horoscope, the crossword, and all the rest, what do you have left? Ten percent of available space for news?

I will even accept the notion that we're simply qualified hacks, if that's what you want to describe yourself as being, and I'll accept the notion that the organization of journalism today is such that you cannot ask of it those things that Bill Greider says ought to be asked of it.

That is not the same thing as saying, however, that it is outside either the intellectual or economic capacity of newspapers to do precisely what Bill is asking. It is the ultimate cop-out to say that if I describe the current reality to you I can't do more of what has to be done.

EVANS: There's another question that perhaps somebody can answer. If, for instance, Dick Harwood put out the *Washington Post* without 10 percent of political sediment, would anybody buy the paper? Is it the repetitive, the daily expectation, the addiction to the news that makes readers buy the paper, including the home and the style sections and the classified ads?

Professor Lanson has some observations about one of the undercurrents of the Greider thesis, which is the need for more interpretation and analysis and retrospection.

GERALD LANSON: I want to start by saying I think Bill Greider raises some significant points about the problems of press coverage. I think the press is preoccupied with what happened yesterday. It can't forget that while it has to be a daily chronicler of events, there is room to look back.

The press also is at times obsessed with predictions. Journalists in general are gamblers and they like the idea of looking ahead: Who's going to win the next election? Who'll be the Democratic nominee?

Thirdly, the press too often does forget context, forgets to have any sense of continuity. It forgets to mention that Ronald Reagan was promising a balanced budget by 1984. It's something the public should not be allowed to forget.

There has been a tendency, although the press is getting smarter in terms of economic coverage, to accept claims at face value. There is a tendency not to add up the figures, a tendency to say the budget deficit will be $60 billion without any explanation of those figures.

I also think there is too much reliance on insiders, those people in government who are putting the figures together. There's been a lot of argument about backgrounders, and whether we should know who within the government is putting the figures together. There hasn't been much said about the need to go outside government, to go away from the people putting together the figures, and to talk to people in universities, Congress, businessmen who could provide some perspective on the record.

I disagree, probably fairly strongly, with Bill Greider on the question of solutions to the problems. It's possible to improve the quality of reporting without changing its nature. The press can do a better job of presenting what is knowable, the facts.

I jotted down three stories where the facts could give you a good idea of what was going on.

Had the Reagan tax machinations put money in one pocket and taken more from another pocket? In other words, first we had a tax cut and then we had user fees being piled one upon another. Could you look back and put some of those figures together?

How have the massive cutbacks, the staffing cutbacks in agencies, affected enforcement of existing laws? Record keeping? The availability of information? Again, it takes investigation. It takes time. But I think a lot of information is factual, on the record and can be put together. I'm not saying the press has not done this at all. I'm saying I'd like to see more of this kind of story.

A tougher one is why has the energy crisis evaporated? And will it return?

Bill (Greider) suggests that the press should try to make sense of things for its readers. I think he's saying that we're responsible for what people understand. He stops short of saying the press should tell readers its version of the truth in news stories as well as in analysis or in op ed pieces, but I'm not so sure he stops far short of that.

There's a bit of irony in this point of view. He suggests that public policy is disordered, that it's helter skelter, that no one in Washington really knows what's happening. Yet he calls on the press to do what the politicians apparently cannot do, which is to penetrate chaos and tell us what is really going on. I have to ask, if the people elected to the office, the people who deal with the same story day in and day out can't sort it out, is an average reporter intelligent enough to do what those people can't do?

To encourage, indeed to expect daily journalists to do this, invites guesswork. At times it also redirects the focus of articles away from the news. Reporters can give us glimpses of personalities while they're trying to sort out who's really in control this week and why. You sometimes get situations in which what is happening and how it affects us becomes obscure. There's a danger that in calling on people to come up with the "why," we lose sight of what happened.

If we start confusing our readers, if we start muddling facts with interpretation, I, as a reader, will feel cheated. I'd like the right to read things and come to my own conclusion of what the truth is. I know whom I trust and whom I don't trust. I'd like to have the right to sort out what the different people are saying, what is the information, what facts are there.

Let me throw out some questions, since that's really what we're doing here. Why should we trust journalists? Don't they participate in off-the-record briefings and private discussions with sources? Aren't they subject to the same kind of manipulations as everyone else? Don't they, in rubbing elbows every day with important people, begin to think of themselves as famous and important? Don't they, to some extent, lose perspective on what's going on away from the Hill?

Why should we trust journalists? Haven't journalists been taught not to trust institutions, even the presidency? Why should the public believe that the institutions journalists work for are holier than the institutions of their elected officials?

Can even the best reporter, given three or four hours to digest the news, interpret it thoroughly and accurately in what often is three or four paragraphs? How often does the press have room for something that is not brief and pithy? Why should we trust the White House reporter who writes about defense and economics and education and social services and any number of issues and must be an expert on all of them? Isn't this a superhuman task? Doesn't the specialist, the specialized reporter in business or labor, face the same pressure as cabinet officers, of gradually being co-opted to a narrow point of view?

I think the objective tradition is no more than a guidepost. No one claims that pure objectivity is possible. It's a good guidepost, because it forces reporters to test their own biases. The objective tradition also reminds reporters that they are chiefly around to inform people as fully as they can, so people can arrive at their own conclusions of what truth is, rather than having reporters tell them what truth is. It keeps reporters from saying, "Forget what the guys you elected are telling you. Let me tell you what's really going on."

ROY PETER CLARK: I want to offer a pro-Greider thesis if I may. When I was a boy my grandfather used to take me to the old Madison Square Garden to watch prize fights. I enjoyed boxing, and enjoyed reading about it in the *New York Daily News*. The *News* would sometimes carry round-by-round descriptions of important fights. Those descriptions provided me with details of the fight, told without elaboration and in fragmented time. "He's up. He's down. He's up. He's down."

What was missing, of course, was the blood, sweat, spit, muscle, and strength. The narrative of the fight. Other writers provided that, and I turned to them with great pleasure.

I open with this memory, for I believe that the stream of daily stories on the economy is equivalent to the round-by-round synopsis of the fight. Imagine reading about a prize fight one round per day for 15 days. What you miss is the moral weight of the narrative, the story of the game.

It is William Greider who provides us with that narrative on the budget process, and it is the form of his story and the character and quality of the reporting and the writing which made it, in Greider's own words, a "notorious article" we have come here to study.

It may be helpful to remember Joan Didion's introduction to her book, *The White Album*: "We tell ourselves stories in order to live." She writes, "The princess is caged in the consulate, the man with the candy will lead the children into the sea. We look for the sermon in the suicide, the social or moral lesson in the murder of five." We may think that we're reporting the news, but we are also, especially when we rely upon narrative, communicating values to the reader. We are contributing to the collective memory of an otherwise fragmented society. We are doing, to overstate it grossly, what poets used to do.

Greider had a hint about the power of his own narrative when he said in his introduction, "These stories of doubt and misgivings and policy battles had in fact been printed in the newspapers, but clearly they were not told in a way that made much impression outside the inner circle."

We can learn much from the way Greider tells his story, at least until page 69 when he shifts from narrative to essay.

Such a rhetorical analysis reveals the inadequacies of those daily bulletins about the economy which appear in most of our newspapers. Greider understands the budget as a human document, writes about it as such and in so doing makes it understandable and appealing to readers. He illustrates that the budget means citizens vying for the limited resources of government. Contrast Greider's language, if you will, to cliches of economic reporting which blight the daily bulletins. I'm talking about the chopping blocks, the bottom lines, the tightened belts, the rate boosts, the purse strings, the guns and butter school of writing.

Nor does Greider assume that his readers know what entitlement programs are, or the difference between categorical grants and block grants. I dare you, for example, to read the daily bulletins, close your eyes, and not envision the budget as something that looks like a pizza.

My second point is that Greider's narrative treats politicians as human characters rather than figures of authority. Stockman is the most human character of them all. Listen to the souped up language of the publisher's note which introduces the book: " 'The Education of David Stockman' is a narrative of political action with overtones of tragedy, as the idealistic young conservative reformer discovers the complexities of the political system and watches as his moral principles are undermined by the necessities of compromise."

That's "dust-jacket-blurb" talk, folks. You know you're in for something when an introduction to a book on the budget contains Sophoclean imagery.

Stockman is alive and real. He has roots, he thinks, connives, hopes, and backtracks. He eats. He slams his papers down on his desk and waves away associates. I have this vision of readers all over America cheering because, by God, a bureaucrat is behaving in the active voice.

Let's consider the way Greider uses quotations. Either through effective interviewing, or through great patience and selectivity, he's able to evoke quotes which explain, enlighten, and reflect character. Stockman says, "Let's say that you and I walked outside and I waved a wand and said, 'I've just lowered the temperature from 110 to 78.' Would you believe me?" The quotes in the daily bulletin stories come from talking heads, authorities popping out of boxes, rather than human characters, or they are the predictable responses of special interests or political adversaries.

"The American people want action," Congressman Latta tells the House.

I must say that I could barely read some of the stories in the packet of stories we were given, and I must say that Bart Rowen's columns shone like bright jewels among some of the writing.

It seems to take three readings for me to understand a lead and a symbolic month to wade through some paragraphs. Contrast this to Greider's lead, and consider its rhetorical effect and the images it evokes for the reader. We begin with David Stockman at his farmhouse in western Michigan. He was reared there, and we catch him in a reminiscence about traditional American values. He evokes "a youthful world of hard work, variety, and manageable challenges."

It is American Pastoral, the Golden Age, and Greider's language is lyrical: "A light snow had fallen the day before, dusting the fields and orchards with white, which softened the dour outline of the Stockman brick farmhouse." Something violates the serenity of this scene, along with Stockman's sensibilities, "a minor anomaly in the idyllic world landscape: two tennis courts built with federal money." That concrete detail helps us enter Stockman's mind and heart, and it gives us direct access to his economic theory. Throughout the article, the writer effectively climbs up and down the ladder of abstraction, to use Senator Hayakawa's semantic image. He puts facts and details in context and he illustrates generalizations.

Next, Greider establishes authority for the reader by giving us inside information, or what seems like inside information, a sense of the real skinny, the stuff that reporters know but rarely put into stories.

The best example is "the magic asterisk." He also ties the narrative together with recurring words and phrases—"Who knows?" "It's out of control." "It's the

way the world works." "John Anderson's questions."
There are many rhetorical devices in his toolbox: the
analogy, the metaphor, the microcosm.

Certainly length is a factor. The length of the
narrative permits Greider to control the pace for his
readers. Complex information comes in digestible
chunks. Passages that are BBI—"Boring, But
Important"—are followed by interesting quotes or
anecdotes which reward the reader. He introduces
difficult concepts gradually, provides history in context.
The reader learns it, caught up in the narrative.

This contrasts with what I call the "dense pack"
school of writing—which attempts to cluster as much
information, jargon, and statistical confusion into a
paragraph as possible.

As a reader, I've come to distrust with Professor
Lanson the prognostication embedded in daily
newspaper bulletins. They fail to come true often
enough to make a skeptic of any reader.

Greider has the benefit of hindsight. He can judge
results, sources are clear, attribution is ample, his
narrative has weight and authority. In short, as
narrator, Greider has given his story something which
scholars of language and writing call "voice," the
illusion of a voice speaking directly to me, the reader.
It is the voice of an informed, concerned, sincere
character. I'll just ask you to remember that the words
author, authentic, and *authority* come from the same
root.

To achieve this voice, the narrator must have a
sure sense of audience. The daily bulletins read as if
they were written for accountants or computers—at
least some of them do. Greider is writing for me, an
educated reader who knows very little about the
budget but who would like to know more.

He understands that writing is a transaction
between writer and reader, that there is no substitute
for in-depth reporting and effective writing, and if
those are considered innovations, Lord help us.

LANSON: Let me make one response. That was
beautifully written. I think, though, you were talking

about the effectiveness of Bill Greider as a writer, and you're not pointing out one major point. I don't know if it's been addressed today. Bill Greider had nine months to follow this story. He had an inside source and he could look back after nine months and put the entire narrative together. Daily journalists don't have that luxury. They're forced on a day-to-day basis to try to put some meaning into stories. If they were to take nine months and then look back, I think they would succeed.

ZUCKERMAN: Nor do they have 25,000 words. When an excerpt was printed in the *Post,* it took a page and a little bit. You can't get that kind of space in any daily newspaper, so you condense things. You do have to dense pack.

ROWEN: I wanted to respond to a couple of points, very important points, that Gerald Lanson raised.

Why trust journalists, he asked. Can't they be co-opted? Why should we follow their interpretation? How can a White House reporter be an expert on defense, economy, strategy, all those. I think those are very good questions. Obviously you can't trust all. Some journalists can be co-opted and some journalists, as Hodding has said, visualize themselves as assistant secretaries of state when they're covering the State Department.

I know one former correspondent for the *New York Times* who did not write a very significant international economic story because he felt it was not in the interests of the United States to see that story in print. That is not an isolated example, although it's probably the worst one I know of.

I think there is no choice except to trust reporters to be interpretive, to get more interpretive stories into the paper. I agree with Bill fully. We have to do more interpretive reporting, or we might just as well do what the Tass guy does and ship all the garbage out, all of the so-called facts generated and regurgitated by government departments.

That is our function, and if a legitimate question can be raised as to why we should trust these guys, then it's a function for all of us to ask, what is it we're doing well enough? What is it that we have to do in order to provide a better, more steady diet of contextual reporting?

It isn't a question of why we should trust journalists to do this. The question is, how can we improve the process and get it done better? There is no alternative if we have any function.

GREIDER: The overwhelming advantage I had was that I was doing a narrative in just an absolutely fundamental sense. It was a story with a beginning, a middle and an end, and that was, to use an immodest phrase, a work of artifice, because I appreciate fully that from this incoherent mountain of facts, information and impressions, I had to construct a narrative.

My only argument would be, for those who think it's a dangerous thing to mix narrative with news, that there's a different format for writing a standard news story, which is also a work of artifice. I don't think one has a higher sense of reality, necessarily, than the other.

CARTER: If it is important from the perspective of some of us to reveal that government is, in fact, the Wizard of Oz and pull back that curtain, the other side is that there should be an exercise for those who practice journalism. This useful exercise would be to say every day, "Frankly, folks, you should not trust us to be telling you the ultimate truth. We are doing the best we can today. What you are getting is our approximation today of what we understand it to be. It's not the way it is, but it's the best we've done today."

The Public View

HAROLD EVANS: As an opening speaker for this afternoon's session, I have asked Kermit Lansner, who as you know is a former editor of *Newsweek* as well as a pollster, to comment on the evidence of the polls.

KERMIT LANSNER: Polling and journalism have at least one thing in common. At their best, both convey a sense of immediacy, of what is going on at a given time. But they both age badly. Even the best journalism does not turn into history. It can be one source for historical research, but anyone who has thumbed through old clips has had to bring his own excitement to the task. Old stories fade away.

Polling results are even more perishable. Coming out of the field with the latest findings in hand, a pollster can usually capture his audience whether the subject is market research or presidential pairings or how the public is reacting to the Israeli invasion of Lebanon. But the material is quickly dated. At best it turns into a point on a trend line. At worst it can become irrelevant.

Which is to say that you will have to bear with me. I have taken Harold Evans' assignment quite literally. He asked me to "tell us the public perception of the budget and related economic issues from public polling material." One of Greider's main contentions is that it took the public a long time to realize that there was anything wrong with the budget, which was to produce huge deficits, and that the press generally disregarded the predictions and warnings of April and May 1981. So I have had to go back and look at some of our findings about those public attitudes which not only change from week to week, but are so often contradictory.

First let me drop back to 1980, the year of the election. As in every presidential campaign the pollsters were out in force, tracking every nuance of public feeling about the campaign itself, and also about the economic and political situation generally. I would like to sum up the findings of a substantial study on the economy that the Louis Harris firm did that year. As of March 1980 people were obsessed with the problem of inflation (67 percent mentioned it as the most serious problem facing the nation; 80 percent thought that prices were rising more rapidly than the year before); moreover, the public continued to think, as it had for the previous five years, that the country was in a recession. Indeed, about one-third of the public saw a good chance of a depression in the next five years. At one point we asked the public to define a depression. The answers had nothing to do with a falling GNP, but offered rather a vision of failing banks, foreclosures, mass unemployment, business failures and scenes of economic despair—images one can often find in late night reruns of old movies, or on the 7 o'clock news just a few days ago.

I might also point out that the public uses the word recession in a special way. For them it is something like Arthur Okun's "Discomfort Index," a mix of inflation and unemployment plus the sheer personal difficulty of making ends meet. So whatever the official figures say, ordinary people have felt that the nation was in a recession for a long time.

Moreover, and here we will begin forging our link with the Stockman affair, the public has certain views about the dynamics of the economic situation. Although eight out of 10 thought energy prices, OPEC and the big oil companies were the main causes of inflation, almost as many blamed federal spending or, to put it another way, "the federal government spending more than it receives in taxes." Since the energy problem looked insoluble at the time, people wanted to cut government spending to control inflation. Their favorite method of doing it was wage and price controls.

Now people are always for cuts in federal spending to control inflation, but their feelings in 1980 were particularly strong. By 84-to-11 percent they supported cutbacks in general. The difficulties came with the specifics. The fact was that majorities wanted no cuts at all or an increase in defense spending, aid to education, mass transportation, Social Security payments and health care.

More to the point, a 2-to-1 majority agreed with the argument that the country would have to go through a recession to slow down the rate of inflation; and 55 percent said they would favor measures that would bring on a recession if they could be sure it would slow down inflation. Union members and business executives saw almost eye-to-eye on this matter, as they did on the necessity of going through a recession. In retrospect, one can say they didn't quite realize what they were bargaining for.

One more thing—taxes. Our question was put rather carefully and the public was asked to take into account the "current economic, political and international situation." We found that 48 percent wanted personal income taxes decreased, but 43 percent wanted them left the same. People felt somewhat more positive about business corporations with 15 percent opting for a decrease, 37 percent an increase, and 32 percent for the status quo. Clearly Ronald Reagan's pollster was charting the same findings as other pollsters and the Republicans were using the findings quite effectively.

For the record, let me tick off where the public stood in the election year of 1980 on some of the issues that were central to the presidential campaign:

• People were obsessed with inflation, though there is some evidence that their anxiety had peaked, for they saw it lessening a year ahead as a result of some of the proposals that President Carter had made. As a footnote one might note again that the public's preferred approach to throttling inflation was wage and price controls, which only Richard Nixon, among recent presidents, had the temerity to propose.

• People wanted a stronger defense. They were shocked by the Afghanistan invasion and humiliated by the Iranian affair. But they were not particularly jingoistic and they still had their reservations about massive rearming.

• People wanted lower taxes. But as we have seen they did not go overboard on this and they had the good common sense to know that someone has to pay for government services.

• Most importantly, people seemed to be all for a
cutback in the size and powers of the federal
government which seemed to have become too vast,
too intrusive and too inefficient. This implied a cut
in federal spending, and people were all for that. But
as I have noted, they were very choosy about where
these spending cuts should take place.

Another theme which came to the fore was the
public's desire to "revitalize" American industry, to
use the jargon of the day. People were worried about
the decline in industrial productivity, in technological
innovation and development, and in the weakened
competitive position of the United States in world
markets. On the other hand, the public had not
become particularly protectionist. They saw trade as
a two-way street and they knew that as consumers
they benefited from import competition.

More importantly, the American people wanted
a change in national leadership. Polling data, not to
speak of ordinary observation, pictured a presidency
that was indecisive, introverted, depressed and
unlucky. This may have been the prime reason for
the election of Ronald Reagan.

As you know, presidential campaigns are also
periods of intensive public education. As a
counterpoint to the rhetoric, the bombast and
buffoonery, the carefully calculated performances of
the candidates, the media carry on an intense
commentary on issues. A peculiarity of the last
campaign was the vigorous introduction of ideological
positions, both by the Moral Majority on the social
side and the so-called supply-siders on the economic
side. From the beginning there was an enormous fuss
about these positions and great expectations were
roused by the fervor with which various ideas were
pushed.

If I were asked whether the American people were
any more in the dark about Reagan's economic
program than they usually are about complex
economic matters, I would have to say, no, they were
not. Reagan had no hidden agenda. It was all out there
in the open. So we arrive at the early days of 1981,

the beginning of the Reagan administration, the start of a new economic era and the first conversations between William Greider and David Stockman. By this time in the educational process which is a presidential campaign, people had heard about Kemp-Roth supply-side economics, and even the death of Keynesianism. They were quite aware of the overall thrust of Reaganomics, which was not so much a theory as a political program. Of course they were not familiar with any of these economic ideas in an intimate way, but, after all, who is except for professionals in the field?

Looking back to the Harris surveys of early 1981 (surveys which Stockman undoubtedly saw) one finds that the public continued to express its support for selective federal spending cuts, and as I have noted before there was a conspicuous absence of charity in the public's view of where the ax should fall. Medicare, Social Security and veterans' benefits were inviolate, as were child nutrition programs, aid to education, and Medicaid to a lesser degree. Vulnerable were such things as CETA, food stamps for low income people, community development programs and welfare payment grants, to mention only a few.

By the end of January 1981 the public had begun to see some of the problems inherent in a program that wanted to cut taxes and spending at the same time. In fact they rejected the idea of simultaneous cuts by about 2-to-1 and felt that "there should be no tax cuts until federal spending had been cut in a major way."

I have dwelt at length on the public's original skepticism about the president's two-edged ax because it seems to show an understanding of the problems inherent in this approach. But when the administration launched its full court press on the budget and the president used his skills as a communicator to speak directly to the American people, there was little disbelief. Not only did a 72-to-25 percent majority favor the president's proposal to increase the military budget by $7 billion, but they supported all the other major cuts proposed by the president except for cuts in federal aid to education and in Medicaid.

In the burst of surveys that were published after the president's February 18 address to Congress and after the intense propaganda campaign conducted in behalf of his program, there were some significant findings. First, the previous concern about simultaneous tax cuts and spending cuts seemed to have vanished. By 65-to-31 percent, people favored the president's proposal for a 10 percent cut in the federal income tax rate every year for the next three years. Kemp-Roth was alive and kicking. And I might say the public favored the idea even though the survey question used embodied the thought that "some people think this will be inflationary and favor the rich, but others think this will stimulate economic growth."

The public also pulled out the stops in support of a slew of other tax cutting measures that had not been mentioned in Reagan's speech. By 3 and 4-to-1, people were all for speeding up depreciation write-offs for new plants, for reducing the maximum tax rate that individuals pay on non-salary income from 70 to 50 percent, for reducing the capital gains tax and for increasing investment tax credits.

By and large, in the wake of the budget message, a majority of Americans also seemed to think that the Reagan economic program was "fair and equitable" for most groups in the country. However there was a feeling that it was unfair to the elderly and those on pensions and a substantial number of people thought that the program went too easy on big business and high income people, particularly the latter.

Of course, what a 69-to-25 percent majority of the public *did not* believe was that "the federal budget would be balanced by 1984," but the deficit had not become the centerpiece of the discussion at that time.

As congressional theater goes, that period between the first budget message and the passage of the Reagan tax bill was extraordinarily lively and many observers sounded more like theater critics than political analysts as they reported on the stage business.

Yet this highly elaborate budget game clearly had an impact on the public. The proposals that the president made were so dramatic and such a departure from the past that they were bound to catch the public's attention.

We were out in the field during the few days before the March 30 attempt on the president's life and that survey is worth noting. It is rather equivocal, but it shows a continued pessimism about the future of the economy. Most conspicious was the public's emphatic view that the "rate of inflation will not have come down below 10 percent a year from now." They were almost as pessimistic about interest rates. On the prospects for more and better jobs, greater economic growth and lower mortgages, the public was about evenly split.

To indicate how tricky some of these findings are, I would like to give you the responses to a comparable question which was asked in a long survey on the economy and taxation carried out between April 11 and April 26. Sympathy and admiration for a wounded president, the way the question was worded, and the context in which it was asked resulted in much more upbeat answers than those from the survey that I have just quoted. By 64-to-28 percent, the public thought that "if Congress approves what the administration proposed, the program will reduce inflation." Majorities also thought that the program would increase productivity, reduce unemployment and make U.S. industry more competitive with foreign industry.

By all accounts, the president's televised address on April 28 was a huge success and it triggered the relentless push toward passage of the administration-supported budget bill that was finally to take place. What should be noted in the findings of the economic surveys that were done in the two weeks following the president's triumphant return to action was a decline in the feeling that the president's "new economic policies" would be "fair and equitable," a phrase the Harris survey has continually used. To put it differently, there were noticeable increases, not dramatic but clearly noticeable, in the number of those who thought the program would be unfair and, in particular, that it was "too easy" on big business and high income people. This, of course, was important political data, but it was to be some time before it had a real effect.

At the same time, our surveys were probing opinions on taxes. As always views were mixed and often contradictory. On a personal and pragmatic basis people were heavily in favor of tax cuts, primarily because they saw themselves the victims of bracket creep (85 percent took this view). By 67-to-32 percent, people agreed that the "right tax cuts are those designed to stimulate investment and savings but not to increase consumer spending, which would make inflation go still higher." By 57-to-37 percent, they also felt that "if taxes are cut too sharply then the federal deficit will go up and that would be inflationary." The thinnest margin of support (50-to-42 percent) was reserved for Kemp-Roth, the keystone of the president's program: "By cutting personal taxes 30 percent over a three-year period, the economy will be stimulated so much that the federal government will end up with even more money to pay for federal programs on the defense and social areas."

May 1980 was marked by alarms and excursions on the Hill as Republicans and Democrats kept up the high drama of trying to fashion a budget resolution. But as Greider points out, a "turning point, which Stockman did not grasp at the time, came in May, shortly after the first House victory. Buoyed by the momentum, the White House put forward, with inadequate political soundings, the Stockman plan for Social Security reform." Greider discusses the role that Stockman thought his Social Security proposals would play in reducing the deficit and it is a fascinating part of his piece. He also points out how Stockman misjudged the political kickback.

How did the public react to the administration's Social Security suggestions? To begin with, people were strongly opposed to proposals to cut back benefits and to discourage early retirement. Fifty-three percent were convinced that the system was close to bankruptcy, but 40 percent saw the administration's claims as scare tactics. To the basic question: "How much do you think President Reagan is really committed to keeping the basic Social Security system going," 44 percent said "only some or hardly at all."

Moreover, and this could well have been caused by the Social Security flap, there was a small increase in pessimism about economic prospects in this period. Apprehension about unemployment was growing, and any idea that the budget might be balanced was receding. The country continued to be pessimistic in its perceptions about the future of interest rates and inflation.

What also happened in the early part of June, partly as a result of the Social Security gaff and partly because of the constant discussion of the budget, was an increase in the number of those who felt that the president's program would be unfair to the elderly and the poor, although a 54-to-39 percent majority still felt that the president's "new economic policies" would be fair to "people like you and your family." From June through the middle of August, during the period when the most intense discussions about the budget and the tax bill were still going on, people's sense of the equity of the Reagan program changed little.

As of the beginning of June, sentiment was still running strong for large budget cuts to bring down inflation, but less so for a "big multi-year cut in federal personal income taxes." And the administration was already making adjustments in the fundamental Kemp-Roth proposal which the president had consistently supported.

I have no other data to offer for that period which ends with the passage of the Christmas-tree tax bill and the House/Senate vote on the reconciliation bill. But immediately after these two stunning pieces of legislation, we asked the public about its economic expectations a year from now. They were not much changed from the findings of early June; perhaps a bit more optimistic. Let me go over them again for this, in effect, was the bottom line of the extraordinary process that had gone on between the president's inauguration and the passage of the tax bill.

By 75-to-21 percent, the public thought that the "rich and big business will be much better off" a year from now. This may well have been a simple statement of fact and not a judgment. I really don't think people were terribly exercised by this.

By 64-to-32 percent, they felt that the "poor and the handicapped will be especially hard hit."

By 59-to-33 percent, people thought that productivity would be rising steadily. But productivity is one of those conceptual birds that are hard to get a fix on.

As for the federal budget, a 54-to-38 percent majority thought it would be on its way to being balanced.

We can say the same about the public's 52-to-38 percent prediction that "investment for economic growth would be sharply up." Given the extensive tax cuts for business this seemed logical, and in retrospect it seems rather remarkable that as many as 38 percent thought that investment would not be up.

There was somewhat less optimism about the economy in general with a 47-to-44 percent plurality seeing it expanding at a healthy rate.

Skepticism about the unemployment picture persisted. By 49-to-44 percent, people did not think employment would be reduced in a year; they felt the same way about mortgage rates.

Where the public was grievously wrong was in their expectation that the "rate of inflation would *not* come down to below 10 percent." A 55-to-35 percent majority took this pessimistic view.

And by 63-to-31 percent, the public did not think that interest rates would be down sharply by August 1982.

Here we were at the moment of the administration's greatest success in passing economic legislation that was a small revolution, and the public offered two cheers at best. If the expectations of the public were as important to the future of the economy as some administration theorists thought, this muted applause was not a good omen.

Just after the passage of the tax bill and the budget, the public was surveyed on the question of defense. Here are the findings: 34 percent were for increasing defense spending by the full 7 percent that President Reagan had requested, 24 percent were for increasing defense spending, but by less than 7 percent, 22 percent were for no increase, and 16 percent wanted to cut spending. In sum, 58-to-38 percent majority favored an increase.

To be sure, people were worried about cost overruns and impractical new weapons and too much money sloshing around the whole military system. But they felt that the country had to keep up with the Soviet build-up, and by 73-to-25 percent, they agreed that "President Reagan is right when he says the only way for the U.S. to have peace is to have a military defense second to none." Our survey went on to pose the fundamental question about defense spending as it relates to overall government expenditures. "If the only way to have a chance to balance the federal budget by 1984 was to make sharp cuts in defense spending, would you favor certain defense spending, or would you favor *not* balancing the budget?" This was the question we asked and the answer was forthright. By 63-to-32 percent, people said that they would favor *not* balancing the federal budget.

There are intimations of the problems that the president is now facing in the public's answer to a comparable question: "If the only way to have a chance to balance the federal budget by 1984 was to make sharp cuts in Social Security benefits, would you favor cutting Social Security or would you favor *not* balancing the budget?" By 76-to-17 percent people chose the latter course.

By November 1981, the two cheers had shrunk to one. A majority of 62-to-27 percent felt that in a year inflation would not have come down to below 10 percent. By 59-to-34 percent, those polled thought interest rates would not come down sharply. A 59-to-35 percent majority was convinced that in the next 12 months unemployment would not be reduced to below its then current levels. A 52-to-41 percent majority was convinced that the federal budget would not be on the way to being balanced. And 52 percent, as against 38 percent, felt that the economy would not be expanding at a healthy rate in November 1982.

A Harris report on the poll concluded with this assessment: "For the present, the outlook is gloomy. And that condition usually means trouble for the party that is occupying the White House."

JAMES DAVID BARBER: One of the things we were talking about this morning, and it was a point raised by Bill Greider in his essay, was the blizzard of information that hits us daily and leaves the public undernourished and unaware.

But my reading of these things as I listen to you is, they knew what was happening. They did not respond in a totally ignorant or benighted way. They were making some close choices. What you have here is a prime example, and I've talked to Lou Harris about this, of a fantasy that results from this way of reporting public opinion.

This is one area where you really ought to listen to the academics. We know a lot better than you do what the public really said when you report that by 45-to-35 percent they're in favor of the MX missile as long as it's located in Montana and costs no more than 22.3 percent of the budget. Now, what the public said was, "Huh."

The lady came to the doorstep in a tweed skirt like the League of Women Voters. People are afraid they might not get the answer right, but soon they find out that it doesn't make a bit of difference, so 70 percent have no opinion on anything.

Then we find this reported in the press as if there's some public out there. Of this public, 48 percent don't know there are two senators from each state. And you're asking them whether they're for 7 percent budget cuts or for less than 7 percent budget cuts.

It's bizarre. It really is. You're getting a reflection of global attitudes toward Reagan or toward their own fate. It's particularly insulting to the intelligence when one says they say something strongly, because many of them agreed with the stimulus that Harris presented.

Now, along about 6 o'clock this afternoon, if you polled this group, you might get 80 percent saying they're in favor of dinner. But not one is going to be obsessed with the matter.

In 1980, one of the reasons that the Democrats collapsed in the face of Reagan was the polls. And the academic polls that have come out subsequently show that that mandate was about as empty as it could be.

RICHARD HARWOOD: You're correct in your comments, but I would make the point that from this data, people were making rather subtle distinctions.

BARBER: No, those distinctions were made for them. They didn't make any distinctions.

HOBART ROWEN: I don't want to disagree with my colleague all day long, but I do agree with you. I think also that the questions and the way they were put in a way created a poll that was carrying out the mission of the government.

What else do you expect when you ask, "Would you rather balance the budget or protect the national security?" Would you balance the budget at the expense of a defense budget?

HODDING CARTER: The Democrats deserved to collapse because they had no center and no core of belief, and the American people need somebody who believes something over somebody who's given them a pallid imitation.

It was a lack of guts caused by lack of conviction, and that's what happened in 1981 as far as I'm concerned. Be that as it may, the main trendlines of the polls for 10 years on national defense reflect a very deep and real public conviction. The politicians were reacting to it, and were running to get in front of the crowd. That was no freak phenomenon.

Also, what can only be called the narrow, selfish and "I've got mine, Jack" approach to how we want federal spending cut or retained was not a result of skillful Reagan rhetoric in 1980. It was something which had been building for some time and which crested with this tax bill. It's a reality. It's not something manufactured by bad questions from pollsters in 1981. It's out there. If you don't believe it's out there, go run for office.

LANSNER: I would agree with Hodding. When you ask a simple question such as, do you think you can make ends meet this year, it means nothing unless you ask it over 10 years.

Suddenly you see that the percentage of people who don't think they're going to make ends meet just grows and grows and grows. Then you know something is happening. It's not as if you invented the whole thing.

W. E. (NED) CHILTON: I want to ask David Barber about polls. We run polls in our paper and when I see the other papers run them, I get frantic and think, "We've got to do a poll." Then when I see our poll I say, "Well, that's the stupidest poll I ever saw."

I want to know what you think journalists ought to do and how they ought to construct polls in such a way that they are going to mean something.

BARBER: I think John Robinson is going to deal with some of this later on. The thing that I like best about an academic poll is that we're not afraid to look stupid.

You go to doors and ask, "What are some of the things you like about Reagan?" You really listen to the answers and you take down what they say, not just A to Z. You're really listening to what people are telling you, getting a contact, a sense of priority, their adjectives rather than your adjectives.

When you do that, and you combine it with cognitive questions about their levels of information, an extraordinarily different view of the American public emerges.

EVANS: I've got two members of the public here. They're John Donovan and Mary Margaret Slazas. I asked them before the seminar began to just think basically about what understanding they got from all the headlines and razzmatazz about the budget debate and to comment on anything they've heard today.

Now it's a poll of two, highly unselective, and that's why it's going to be interesting.

JOHN DONOVAN: The man on the street from St. Petersburg would like to have you predict whether President Reagan will run again. I have my own little polling service. I read the dense packed stories about the budget, and they sort of flowed from one year to the other. The mind reels.

I read and reread them carefully, the way you do an IRS form. And the message conveyed to me, as I think it was to a lot of people, was that people are politically illiterate. But even though they couldn't get the percentages right, they smelled a rat. However, when I saw the stories about Stockman himself saying that the whole thing was a hoax, I couldn't believe that he wasn't booted out of office fast. That sort of sideshow confused me. Since then, after listening to various opinions here, I'm in total confusion.

EVANS: Thank you very much, John. That's wonderful. That's a newspaper readership sample of one. Let's see if the other confirms it and make it 100 percent. Mary Margaret Slazas, who is a promotional writer.

MARY MARGARET SLAZAS: I'm glad you're confused, John, because I was, too. I find this a huge subject to digest. The budget is not something I follow with rapt attention, really eager to get on to the next day and find out what's going to happen.

I was very surprised. I don't remember reading it when Reagan began, but he said he was going to balance the budget by 1984. I don't remember reading that, and I was really surprised. I almost laughed when I read it, looking back and seeing where we are today.

I don't think I believed him if he was using this as a campaign promise. I don't think I believed it, so because I didn't believe it, I didn't remember it. And I was surprised to read that. So I continued through the stories, and the numbers and numbers and numbers. Part way through this I remember wondering how I was going to do, sitting up here talking to you, because I wasn't making a lot of sense out of it.

But then I found one piece from the *Washington Post* which said much of it was a numbers game, and Reagan apparently opted for using the smallest possible base for calculating his annual defense increase. Stockman had favored using a fiscal '81 budget figure of $171 billion, while Weinberger wanted to measure further increases against the fiscal '82 figure of $222 billion.

No wonder I don't know what's going on. Everybody wants to use a different base. What percentage is valid? And then when I got to the article on Stockman and his quote, when he said that really, none of us understands what's going on, and nobody seems to know how to control it, then I didn't feel quite as dumb. I don't understand a lot of this and I'm not sure anybody does. I don't honestly believe that we will have the deficit under control any time soon.

HOWELL RAINES: I want to go back to something we talked about this morning, what we knew and what we didn't know, and what readers didn't know even though we had the benefit of all of the stenographic reporting and interpretive reporting about this budget.

What the readers didn't know was that the man who was working on the numbers was juggling them. And what they didn't know was that he was saying that trickle-down economics is the same old thing in a new racket. If that had been told it would have been shocking.

The point I tried to get us to focus on this morning gets back to the question of what the *Post* did with the information it had. It is not the information, it is the voice, the personality speaking the words. That is what gave the Greider piece impact.

EVANS: In fact, a disembodied source is almost meaningless in terms of getting anybody to read the story.

I have been a newspaper editor for 21 years and in the newspaper business for about 35, and I almost never believe spokesman stories, the unsourced stories. I've used them many times myself, but even when I know the guy, when I read it in the paper it doesn't have any credibility.

RAINES: I wonder what it would have meant if you had seen a story that said David Stockman believes these numbers have been juggled to make them look better, and he believes that this is traditional Republican economics that will favor the rich and hurt the middle and lower income types. What would have been your reaction to that?

DONOVAN: My opinion of Reaganomics would have gone down the tube.

RAINES: Mary Margaret, would it have shaken your faith in the Reagan economics program to know that David Stockman had these opinions about it?

SLAZAS: Yes. I didn't have a lot of faith in it to begin with. Like everybody else, I wanted to believe that this man was going to make a difference, even way down the line when he was digging his heels in and saying, we're going to hold on to this, we're going to keep it going, it's not showing yet but we're going to hold on to it and keep working on this program. I don't know whether to admire him or to say, you're too stubborn, give up.

WILLIAM GREIDER: Would you have recognized him as the principal architect of the Reagan program had that been made public at the time? Would you have recognized that Stockman was the guy who was supposed to be carrying it on the Hill and so on?

SLAZAS: Until all this erupted with his saying things he shouldn't have said, I didn't really know who he was.

DONOVAN: I was aware of who he was.

RAINES: This, it seems to me, gets back to the fundamental question of journalistic obligation and journalistic ethics. It was a question that was not answered to my satisfaction in the introductory essay in Bill's book.

To me it did not address sufficiently the question of what obligation the *Post* had to communicate to the public this subversive knowledge that one of its top editors had acquired.

I don't think I have yet heard an argument that is convincing to me that the *Post* as an institution and Bill as a journalist used this knowledge in the blunt, forceful way that it could have been used, and in a timely way.

EVANS: Why didn't the *Post* have it on the front page that the government was constructed on a lie and the whole thing was phoney?

GREIDER: Both the *Times* and the *Post,* to be narrow on that point, had that story. What you're talking about is the numbers that they play with the budget resolutions. That was written at the time. It is true, we didn't have David Stockman saying nobody's resolution is honest. In a more general way, I could trot through the clippings from the first of the year to the end. Some reporters were informed by me, some of them were not. They were just doing their own reporting.

These stories fairly reflected, albeit usually anonymously, the points of controversy. However, I realize that did not have the same impact as when David Stockman said it up front. In my defense, I would say that ultimately, under these ground rules which I believe I honored, I did get those words into print.

RAINES: Back to my original point. There were two elements, it seems to me, that were not communicated to the public. Those were that Stockman was working over the figures, massaging them in what some people thought was a deceptive way, and that trickle-down economics had been disguised as supply-side. I don't think the public knew that. I think you, Greider, knew it in advance of us.

We all know when you take off-the-record information you potentially put yourself in an ethical box. You know things that the public ought to know that you can't tell them.

What I'm suggesting is that this matter is of such magnitude, and it's so subversive and so explosive in terms of political and public opinion that I'm wondering why the *Post* didn't figure out a way to purge it of its off-the-record commitment.

EVANS: That's a good question. How far do you have to go before you indulge in betrayal?

I once asked my best investigative reporter, what is the secret of investigative journalism? And he said, the art of betrayal.

If, for instance, you learn that the president is lying in the White House, how many people would keep a secret of the source? And at what point does the public obligation override this ethic which we've set up as a personal ethic?

We turn now to Mortimer Zuckerman. I put him down for the businessman's point of view.

MORTIMER ZUCKERMAN: What I was going to do is spend a few moments talking about business news or economic news, not in terms of the daily transaction price for IBM stock or copper futures or what have you, but taking a somewhat larger perspective.

The sort of issues I'm talking about include the budget, the budget deficit and its impact, monetary policy and the issue I would describe as being more relevant today, the international financial crisis.

Here you have a very complicated issue. Many responsible people who understand that and who spend a lot of time on it, say it may very well collapse the Western financial system. And how does the media convey not only the facts, but the narrative and the urgency of it all?

You have a situation which has emerged over a period of five or six years, not something that's happened overnight. What would have happened if the Mexican president had decided to declare a moratorium, or had done what Argentina just did, say they would pay off the next $5 billion development debt with Argentinian bonds, which as you know are in sharp demand for wallpaper. The system could have collapsed.

I happened to pick this issue because on the cover of this week's *Time* magazine is the "debt bomb."

Yesterday's *Wall Street Journal* had a story about bankers which said they're resolving the issue by not only lending the money which they owe for interest and principal, but even more money which is just going to deepen the problem.

EVANS: May I just stop you for a minute? This morning Gene Patterson mentioned blood and chaos in government.

If we blow this story up to front-page headlines and there's a run on the banks, we precipitate the very crisis you're talking about.

ZUCKERMAN: Exactly right. I think that is the problem. How do you convey this when it might become a self-fulfilling prophecy? If the banking system rests on confidence, and the media suddenly start talking about this issue, what happens?

What is the obligation here? Who makes these judgments? What does the journalist do in this case? And does he allow it to go on, as the *Wall Street Journal* editorializes, in such a way that he deepens the problem and creates the condition for a larger collapse?

How do you find a way, if you feel it is urgent, to convey "banks in trouble" to the public? How could you convey it in a way that would capture some kind of dramatic attention? Bill was able to do the Stockman story because he had Stockman's quotes. Who would you quote here?

How do you write some form of narrative that deals with the particular urgency of the problem? The media are much better at conveying revolution than evolution.

LANSNER: The reassuring thing is that the media always get to it after the thing is past its peak. People have been talking about this story now for how long?

ROWEN: The story has been generating for about a year.

CARTER: I want to disagree with that because there was a two-part series in July and August 1976 in the *New York Review of Books* by Emma Rothschild which describes precisely everything which is happening now.

Why wasn't there a major media look then, saying that these things were possible, that some countries were going to be cripples six years later. My point is that the run may occur today because background reporting wasn't done then.

ZUCKERMAN: My point here is that it not only has been in the *New York Review of Books,* it's been in a lot of books and journals in the last five or six years.

But you are dealing with a different kind of media. You're not dealing with the *New York Review of Books,* you're dealing with the *Washington Post,* the *New York Times,* and particularly television and the news weeklies.

How can you convey that kind of story as a kind of narrative that somehow brings its urgency to the public attention?

Are you responsible for doing that? Is there a journalistic or a media responsibility for somehow focusing on this thing?

You had the secretary of the treasury saying in September we will not contribute any additional money to the IMF (International Monetary Fund). Ninety days later, the secretary said we're going to increase IMF funding by 50 percent or $35 billion. You take the $35 billion from U.S. taxpayers and give it to the IMF. The IMF then loans it to Brazil and Mexico and Argentina. They give it directly back to the banks to pay off their loans. So the banks don't show a default, and we all hide behind the illusion and somehow or other we might skate by it.

ROWEN: There's a lot of shorthand going on in your discussion. It's a little oversimplified.

CHILTON: What would happen if the banks did call a default?

ZUCKERMAN: You could have a very quick collapse of the banking system. The banks might not collapse, but you'd have a tremendous contraction of economic activity funded by the banks.

GREIDER: I don't want to interrupt, but that's part of what I alluded to this morning when I said there's an economic cycle of forces, things happening in the world, and a political cycle which only occasionally coincides with it.

The illusion that the political cycle is somehow in control of the economic cycle is part of the mythology that the news media among others ought to take on. I'm sure Bart was writing about this same problem five years ago. Bud (Bernard) Nossiter wrote a series of pieces about the bank loans in Eastern Europe four or five years ago in the *Post*.

It is only as the problem reaches crisis level that the news media turn to government officials and says, you must be in control of this problem, how are you going to solve it?

ZUCKERMAN: You're dealing with projections. People are trying to estimate what might happen. There are all sorts of things happening behind the scenes because there is a national interest or at least a financial interest in preventing anything that might undermine confidence in the banks.

EVANS: So you see the press as being a kind of censoring mechanism?

ZUCKERMAN: What is the role of the press in something like this? How does the press make a judgment that publishing these stories in some kind of a dramatic way won't produce a catastrophe?

ROWEN: What kind of judgment do you think *Time* magazine made by putting that story on its cover? Isn't that giving it a good deal of highlight? I think there's a difference between that and six years ago, and the difference is that this problem has been magnified multifold by the high interest rates resulting from Reaganomics. The problems that we have with the world debt are 10 or 20 times what they were six years ago.

What's happening now is that we're really to the point where interest rates are so high, stagnation is so great, that countries that have borrowed all this money don't have the means of selling their goods to earn money with which to pay it back. Meanwhile, all of the money they're borrowing is just barely paying the interest on what they already owe. They're borrowing money to pay the interest on old debt. That's the kind of situation we're in now, which is totally new. It's a dimension that nobody has even approached before.

In recent weeks we have done at least two major pieces the headlines of which were something like, can the banks survive the gold crisis? I don't view this as a story which has been as subordinated to reality as perhaps the budget story might have been. I think this is a story which is getting a tremendous amount of attention within a reasonable scope.

You also cannot say that everybody with a deposit in a domestic bank is going to be hit if Chase Manhattan's loans to Brazil are defaulted. It's going to hurt Chase stockholders, it's going to hurt David Rockefeller, it's going to hurt a lot of communities. But it isn't necessarily going to have the impact of a default or the demise of a domestic bank.

ZUCKERMAN: To a large extent business people have special publications—*Business Week, Forbes, Fortune.* Then you have the *Wall Street Journal,* which most business people look to as a source of major information. I think the business community, more than any other group, subscribes to the notion that "I'm all right, Jack, you pull up the ladder."

If the business community thought they were going to get a tax cut out of Reagan's program I think 90 percent could care less about a lot of the other economic issues. In the meantime, "just give me the tax cut." I think that is a large part of what accounted for their support of Reagan's program, even when they knew he was going to produce problems later on.

I think the Stockman story shook the confidence of the business community in the Reagan program more than anything else. I think a lot of people wondered why Reagan didn't fire the son-of-a-bitch? But I think a lot of people looked beyond that. I think it did undermine the credibility of that administration's program. And had it happened earlier, there would have been a measurable impact. There's a general sense that very few people writing in the media understand business or economics. In fact, there's a general sense that very few economists understand economics.

There is a sense of loss of that narrative, the loss of that sense of what really happened. There's the "you never met a payroll" syndrome which the business community always throws at the government. Business people tend to look much more skeptically at pro or con discussion on the budget. And I think it was the personal side of this that had the impact.

Reporting Government

OPENING STATEMENTS BY:

Howell Raines
Hodding Carter
Ray Jenkins
Gavyn Davis

HOWELL RAINES: My colleague, Wayne King, is the subject of an apocryphal story. No, he's the subject of a story. It may be apocryphal and it may not. I don't know.

The story is that when he was a student reporter at the University of North Carolina he confronted an official during a racial demonstration and began asking tough questions about the university's racial policies. The official, somewhat defensively and condescendingly, began saying, well, the fact is, this and that. And to the next toughly-put question, he said well, Wayne, the fact is, this and that. Finally Wayne is alleged to have burst out, "Don't tell me about the facts. I want the truth."

I think the objective any of us has in getting into this business is to try to convey to our readers in understandable form the truth as we see it, and as we can prove it to exist.

Jim Carey made the point that he found out more of what appeared to be truthful by talking to reporters than from reading them. I think most of us have probably had the experience I had as a young statehouse reporter when I found that the best political information was usually traded among reporters over drinks. I tried to figure out ways to get that fascinating shop talk, which was often the public business, into print, with no success.

Moving from statehouse coverage to Washington I observed something: Too often in Washington conflicting networks of confidential relationships have developed into a system of *de facto* procedures that put journalists in the position of holding out on the reader.

All of us use confidential sources and try to develop them and protect them. But when they try to use us to promote their policies and political agendas, I think we ought to always keep in mind that our main mission is to try to use them to get information to the people at the proper time for it to be of use.

Certainly we're all indebted to Bill Greider for telling us the Stockman story, but my enjoyment of it would be keener if I could escape the nagging feeling that the real message of this book is that for a time a great newspaper and a group of hardworking journalists got trapped into holding out on their readers, at a critical point in the Reagan administration, information that could have tilted the political balance.

I hasten to add the point I was trying to close on yesterday—that this has been by no means intended as personal criticism of Bill. His reputation is such that neither criticism nor blame from me would have an effect on it. Only Bill and the editors of the *Washington Post* know the full facts. Perhaps if we had those facts, we would have made the same decisions.

The broader point is that Washington journalism has certain conventional practices that are positive inhibitions to telling readers the best available information in the bluntest fashion at the most opportune moment.

This was brought home to me in mid-November, after 10 weeks of campaign coverage. I went back to the White House to cover a story one day. There I saw a familiar scene in which I had been a participant many times in the 18 or 20 months that I was a regular there. A group of reporters, led by an excited TV correspondent, burst into the press room with the television reporter waving a tape recorder. They had been to a photo opportunity. They were excited because the president had spoken.

We clustered around the correspondent. It was one of those cases where I was both participant and observer because 10 weeks in the relative sanity of the campaign trail had given me some distance from this scene.

The president had been asked what his thinking was on a plan to speed up the third income tax cut just when critics were suggesting that the tax program be dismantled. We dutifully wrote down what the president said. The problem was that his words were trivial. Moreover, it was nonsensical trivia.

Suddenly, I was struck by how White House reporters scramble for the silliest scraps of information. I could not feel superior to my colleagues because I was at once a participant and observer. Later that same day I had another experience with this same set of information that I think illustrates another part of this problem.

I got a call from a copy editor who had a question about including in my story the words the president had spoken. Is it fair, she said, to quote the president's offhand comment that may not make sense?

This is the paragraph, as I wrote it, and it's the third from the last paragraph in the jump, well inside the paper:

"The president's only comment on the matter, made during a picture taking session, seemed confusing. 'I think cutting taxes in a recessionary situation such as this one—I mean, of raising taxes, that would be in effect raising taxes,' Mr. Reagan was heard to say in response to a question before his voice trailed off." That's what I wrote.

HAROLD EVANS: Would it have been possible to say the president was talking nonsense?

RAINES: To indulge in a bit of shop talk, I originally used a more perjorative term, nonsensical or something of that nature. I edited it myself to the confusing construction, anticipating the objections that would be raised, and feeling that it was more important to get the quote on the record to be judged by the reader than to get my commentary.

EVANS: Yesterday one interesting line was that the press infuses order on chaos in government. Another was that we don't expose the blood and chaos of government enough.

RAINES: Well, the occasion was that (Senator Howard) Baker and (house minority leader Robert) Michel had come down to tell Reagan that they lacked the votes to speed up the third year tax cuts.

You recall that when the lame duck session began there was a lot of talk about the third year of the tax cut being dismantled. The White House, figuring a good offense is the best defense, said, "You guys want to talk about dismantling; the president wants to speed it up."

As I try to reconstruct the question from memory, it was something about the critics saying that the deficit was so huge he was going to have to raise taxes. Reagan's response was, "I think cutting taxes in a recessionary situation such as this one—I mean, of raising taxes, that would be in effect raising taxes."

HOBART ROWEN: I think it becomes a lot clearer if you accept the fact that he had a mere slip of the tongue. He didn't mean to say cutting taxes initially. He meant to start by saying it would be a question of raising taxes.

If you eliminate that first phrase, and then read what he said, it makes perfectly good sense. He didn't mean to say "tax cut" in that first clause.

RAINES: My next point goes to the question of how often the president speaks in this mode and whether it's fair to quote him on an offhand remark, which is exactly the question the copy editor raised. My response, based on having heard this man speak many times, was that the president talks this way a lot. Is it fair to the American people to protect him from having them find it out in our newspapers?

RAY JENKINS: Let me add one thing. I wrote an editorial which said exactly the same thing that your copy editor said, but it went a bit further. That question was not supposed to be asked. It was asked at a photo opportunity where it was not supposed to be asked, and I can understand why Larry Speakes could get mad as hell.

Under the rules, reporters are not supposed to question the president. This is another violation of the rules that we're talking about.

MORTIMER ZUCKERMAN: I find that to be almost astonishing. It seems to me the point is not when a question is asked, but the ability of the president of the United States to respond to a question in a reasonably intelligible way.

JENKINS: I was raising that in the context of Jimmy Carter who would have given a very clipped and precise answer. But the fact remains that they were not supposed to ask questions during a photo opportunity.

RAINES: I was hoping to avoid a fascinating debate on the ground rules of the photo opportunity, and it seems to me this experience illustrates a couple of additional problems.

One is the tendency of Washington reporters and editors to treat the presidency, and to a lesser extent the Congress and the government in general, in such a way that trivial events are used to create an illusion of competence and control and order.

Two, despite all the talk of the "ritual destruction" of the presidencies of Nixon, Johnson and Carter, there is still a powerful, reflexive, protective mechanism at work within the press. To some degree this is generational. Older reporters tend to be very strongly patriotic optimists. That tends to generate commentary devoted to glorifying the chief executive and his key advisors for no other reason than that they possess power. But even among younger reporters and editors this surge of patriotic optimism amounts to self-policing of their adversarial instincts.

What accounts for this stacking of the deck in favor of the presidency? There are a number of reasons.

One expressed by Richard Reeves has to do with the limitations of conventional journalism. Reeves said that within those limits there is no way to tell the reader that the president had nothing to say today, and said it badly. So we are playing at a game in which our own rules of fairness, objectivity and proper procedure are sometimes a positive inhibition to blunt communication.

A second factor is the co-optive nature of back channel communications in Washington. As I mentioned yesterday, the *St. Petersburg Times* political reporter in the Florida statehouse or in a similar setting for the *Des Moines Register* has a certain amount of muscle to force people to go on the record.

In Washington there are too many outlets for one organ to have that kind of near monopoly. If the *New York Times* or the *Post* or the networks or the news magazines unilaterally refuse to accept ground rule information, the source will go elsewhere.

Having said that, I want to say that Hodding Carter and Gerald Lanson have pointed toward what seems to be ways to reform this co-optive nature of the back-channel process. As Hodding indicated, a militant and lonely refusal to play by those rules will, in time, pay off.

My belief, based on my own experience, is that virtually everything gotten on a background basis can be gotten on the record. You just have to work harder. But this can only happen, as Lanson suggested, if editors have the backbone to tell reporters, "Don't worry about getting beaten on the spoonfed story. Go get me something fresh, original, unpredictable, something that is, by God, news."

I want to reiterate the point I made yesterday. I think reporters are too often identified as the sole custodians of the background process. Reporters are like football linemen: they'll block for the pass or they'll block for the run, but they have to have some protection the morning after.

I think we in the newspaper business are still captives of the old pre-electronic age scoop mentality. The *Post* and the *Times* spend a lot of time in a headline battle over often trivial developments and events that to the general public are arcane. Until we stand up we'll continue to see abuses of the background system like that in the president's Latin American trip.

You'll recall an offhand remark made under "proper" ground rules in which the president seemed to express surprise that Latin America was made up of many individual countries. The State Department then sent out Thomas Enders on background to say that the president did not mean his remarks the way they sounded. In effect, the administration was asking

us in the press to tell the American people that we
had somehow misled them by using the president's
exact words. I think Mr. Enders has every right to
so accuse us. I think he has every right to say the
president speaks nonsense. I think we have every
right to insist that if he's going to say those things
about us and his boss he should say them under his
own name.

When I first came to Washington in January 1981,
I thought there were a lot of very serious problems
in the coverage of Washington. After 22 months the
problems don't seem quite as serious. I think in two
more years I'll feel damn comfortable. So I'm glad I
have this chance to talk to you before my lobotomy.

One of the problems I see is referred to by my
friend Curtis Wilkie of the *Boston Globe* in jesting
reference to a certain cadre of State Department
reporters as "the ambassadors." It's the "Men of
Washington" syndrome. We need more new people in
the capital.

Now I want to move to another point, the problem
of being heard. One of the most fascinating things
about Bill Greider's introductory essay to me was his
surprise at the public reaction to information which
seemed to him to have been pretty well thrashed out.

It's as if the general public had not been listening
to what we were saying. Why not? I recall a wonderful
phrase from Martin Luther King. He said before you
could communicate with Southern segregationists you
had to create a state of readiness. We have seen a
number of stories in which the public response has
lagged behind the reporting because the state of
readiness was not there. Let me give you a few
examples:

• The dismantling of the civil rights structure,
which the *Post* has covered very adequately and
systematically. But as yet, other than civil rights
activists and the black community there is no
apparent awareness of what this administration has
done.

• Reagan's indifference to human suffering, as
evidenced by his dismantling of the social welfare

system to the degree that he's been able to accomplish that. Robert Perrin of the *New York Times* has reported this in intricate detail, but the public is unaware.

• What we called for a time the "Dracula story"—that is, putting in charge of various departments people who were opposed to their missions. I think the *Times, Post* and the networks have reported the Dracula story pretty well, but it has not taken hold.

• The New Federalism is a guise for states rights stories. And then, of course, there's the Jim Watt story. This, I think, is the next one likely to catch hold because Watt is pursuing policies directly opposed to the will of the American people.

In addition, I want to point out two old stories that were suddenly discovered. One, thoroughly reported by all of the major organizations, was the consumer financed natural gas pipeline. This story had been around Washington for months, years, virtually ignored until Bill Moyers did a comprehensive piece on the CBS news. The other story recently rediscovered is the Bulgarian connection. Whether or not it's true I can't say. *Newsweek*, by bringing together all of the apparent facts in a new and comprehensive way, breathed life into a story that had been ignored in somewhat the same way that Bill was suggesting the economic story was ignored.

I think there are ways to stop it. My prescription, such as it is, would be to overthrow the old "today" news format, the kind of stenographic reporting that was appropriate 50 years ago when we were the first givers of news. I think we've got to be strong enough to really let AP and UPI carry the burden of the daily story and go for the broad stories that Gerald Lanson described in some detail yesterday.

I think our business has the capability to do that. Dick Harwood said that he folded Greider's old biweekly column because he couldn't find anybody who could do it. I understand the point he's making, but I don't really believe he means it. I know three reporters on the *Post* who I think could do it. Every paper I know has underemployed reporters who are occupied with stenographic busywork because we are still wedded to the old forms of reporting.

RICHARD HARWOOD: The first point I would make is that if a reporter or if a person—Howell Raines—comes to Washington from St. Petersburg seeking truth and reality, and if he knocks at the White House they'll say, "Well, who the hell are you? You have a press card?" "No, my name is Howell Raines and I'm searching for truth." Well, they'll say, "Go down the street, go to the Library of Congress and search for it."

My point is that if Howell Raines offers a press card at the gate, and says, "I'm Howell Raines of the *New York Times,*" it's a different person, isn't it?

RAINES: Granted. The difference, I think, is the mass of the institution signified by the press card.

HARWOOD: There's an institutional interest in what you do as an agent of the *New York Times.* And there are institutional interests in curbing, restraining, controlling what may be perceived by that institution as wild impulses on the part of some people who are walking around carrying this piece of paper in their hands.

Mary McGrory wrote a column ridiculing Reagan for his statement about black America. She said he had the gall to say it in the presence of Rios Montt, the president of El Salvador. Someone pointed out to her that he is the president of Guatemala. I found it rather interesting that Mary is ridiculing Mr. Reagan, when Mary herself has never been to South America or Central America. She didn't know Guatemala from El Salvador.

She found it rather odd that the president would say these countries are all different. Now, to go back to that fellow walking around with this piece of paper in his hand. He is outraged that they are "dismantling" the civil rights program, and would like to express that outrage, or thinks his newspaper ought to.

Okay. Reagan ran on a platform against busing. When our reporters were dealing with this someone came in and said, "I've got a hell of a story. They're going to intervene in a suit against busing." My reaction was that Reagan was winning another five million votes.

My point is that the baggage or the pictures the reporter carries are not necessarily baggage or pictures that are in consonance with reality. One man's outrage is another man's political gain. So I think this is why there are institutional constraints, and I'm not in any sense making an argument for all of them, or even that those constraints are necessarily right. I just get back to my question of the skillful hack, whose own value system may not be truth.

JAMES CAREY: The institutional control of the reporter is surely there to maintain the credibility of the institution and the capacity of the institution to operate in an effective way. But historically those controls derive from the nature of capitalist enterprise and the need to discipline workers, to keep their habits under control.

JAMES DAVID BARBER: If I hear what Richard Harwood is saying, the implication is that while the individual reporter's view of reality may be exotic, the institution's is not.

Let me indulge in one anecdote that illustrates this. Three or four weeks ago I wrote a piece of truth for Howell Raines' Sunday edition which they titled "Oval Office Aesop." The key sentence was, "Reagan is the first modern president whose contempt for the facts is treated as a charming idiosyncracy."

I got some mail as a result, and one was from a seasoned reporter on a rival paper who said that he had been on to that propensity of Mr. Reagan's in 1975 and had tried to get a story in the *Washington Post.* The first layer of editors told him okay, but then we're going to have to get some equal idiocy from Reagan's opponents so we'll have a certain balance. By the time it got to the editor who's been played by Jason

Robards, he said he didn't think Reagan was serious when he said that, so he wouldn't report it.

Here's my question. How interested are reporters themselves in the factuality of these matters? My impression is that a lot of journalism, institutional journalism, treats information that's at least a day old as material for what they call a morgue. It's dead. Institutions like the *Washington Post* and the *New York Times* are amazingly primitive in their information storage and retrieval capacities.

The grist of what you're dealing with is all kinds of symbolism, feeling and opinion. Television is really upfront here in always asking the question, "How do you feel?"

There's a certain sense in which journalism may be losing interest in the facts and becoming fascinated by symbolic manipulation, sentiment and opinion. So the question about that quotation from Reagan is the question about the state of his mind and not about the state of taxes. Taxes are dull, but Reagan's mind is something.

KERMIT LANSNER: There has to be a certain passion which triggers these stories. Howell mentioned a series of stories, every one of them good, and I think many of them were treated quite well.

Why isn't there interest in a natural gas pipeline or Watt's demolition of the environmental safeguards? These are real factual stories. You have to dig, you have to interview, you have to look at papers, you have to look at them in the context of history and then put them all together.

Somewhere along the line there has to be a feeling, some passion of the moment, to make this a story. I think that spotlight doesn't fall on these. They're not triggered by anything of enormous concern at a given moment. It's a real problem.

GAVYN DAVIS: One of the things you do is to create the impression that Reagan is stupid. If a quote fits into that story, you use it. If it doesn't fit, you throw it out.

If Carter had made that quote you wouldn't have used it. You wouldn't have thought, "Okay, this gives people a better view of what the truth is." The truth, of course, is your own stereotype of the truth. One of the things that we find in reporting on the British economy, especially abroad, is the stereotype about the British economy. It is written in terms of labor difficulties. Trade union issues then qualify as news because they fit that stereotype. Other issues which are every bit as important do not fit. I think there are an infinite number of examples where your selection of what you write is determined by whether it fits your stereotype.

JOHN ROBINSON: It's too bad that Edward Epstein isn't here because in a couple of his books he's made that point, very eloquently and very persuasively.

In the coverage of Vietnam, for example, he makes the point that up to the Tet offensive there was one form of Vietnam reporting. After Tet the story was, we're losing the war, and stories that indicated we were making progress were systematically weeded out.

ROWEN: I just want to go back to one point that Howell made. In effect, do specialists get co-opted? Dick Harwood and I had this discussion 20 years ago. I can see that if somebody covers the State Department for 10 years he may become an ambassador. On the other hand, given the wrong person, somebody at the State Department for 12 months could become an ambassador, too. I think it depends a lot on the person.

Also, it seems to me there are certain areas, certain specializations, where the specialist performs a unique role. It could be science, it could be technology, it could be economics. I would regret seeing an absolute rule that to get the best, straightest coverage there must be a routine rotation of beats.

HODDING CARTER: I think I'd come down in favor of rotation, with one restriction. I do not believe, despite the prevailing wisdom of the business, that you can put a good reporter on any beat and get a good story out of him.

I think it requires a good deal more than that. I'm getting ready to do a story on news coverage of the Soviet Union. What is clear, without any doubt, is that nine-tenths of all the reporting from there is crap. People neither know the language nor the background so they all do the same story. It's a re-inventing of the wheel by each new beat reporter who goes in and does the same half dozen stories all over again.

If you're going to break the beat system, which I think is a good idea, you ought to at least not play the primitive journalist notion that I'm a good journalist so I will go in there and do a good job. At least give the guy or woman six months or a year of some intelligent training.

EVANS: I don't know whether the system prevails in the United States, but in London government correspondents have formed a club. They share information with each other, and this has become institutionalized to the point that the government calls the club together for briefings. As an editor, I must tell you, I've taken strenuous objection to the idea.

They say they can make a lot more calls when they share information, even though they're working for competitive papers. I said that any reporter of mine who joined the club was fired, and I fired one because it seems to me absolutely essential to maintain the individualism of reporters. Otherwise you lose the point of the plurality of the press.

ROWEN: I don't think we have that kind of system here. You tend to have something like that when people are thrown together on buses covering the White House or a political campaign.

EVANS: One of the pernicious things about the system in London is that if you are a loner, a Howell Raines, the other correspondents don't elect you to the club and you cannot attend the official briefings. That's totally bloody pernicious.

HARWOOD: I think that networking is inevitable. But if I could pass a rule it wouldn't be that you can't have your little club, but I would fix the membership. I would prohibit any *Washington Post* reporter from talking to the *New York Times,* CBS, *Newsweek* or *Time.* It has been my experience that the people from the large institutions all get together.

WILLIAM GREIDER: Waxing anecdotal, when covering McGovern in '72, Dick Stout used to insist on dinner every Friday night with the *Time* magazine correspondent. And if *he* didn't insist on it, the *Time* magazine correspondent would insist on dinner with him, because it was Friday night, they were closing both *Time* and *Newsweek* and they wanted to watch each other all evening long.

GERALD LANSON: I'd like to get back to Dick Harwood's statement, which has troubled me. I think (Gavyn) Davis' point is well taken. The press by its choice of quotes, by its choice of what it's going to use, can very easily forge a stereotype. That's the reason for copy desks, the reason for editors, the reason why people have to look at copy very carefully.

I'm also troubled because I think reporters perceive institutional impulse or chumminess with the powers that be. As a result there's a subtle pressure on reporters to stick with sources who don't stray very far from the center, to be satisfied with statements that are somewhat pat and said under somewhat controlled circumstances.

I didn't respond to Ray Jenkins originally because I didn't realize it was a situation in which certain ground rules were set. There are certainly situations where a president answers questions with no ground rules.

What I heard Ray Jenkins say was that if the man isn't prepared you can't ask a question. That seems to me to be contrary to the basic tenets of reporting.

RICHARD STOUT: Just three very minor points which are all obvious and with which all of you are familiar. I offer them just to provide a dollop of historical perspective.

We all know that stereotyping in the press is not at all new. If you go back to the presidential press conferences of Dwight Eisenhower, recall how he used to speak in "Casey Stengalese" language which got a lot of attention from the press.

Then there's the question of whether the *Post* in a *de facto* way held out on the public in some pernicious way in the Stockman story. That's not the first time at all. The classic example is the Bay of Pigs story which the *New York Times* did not print in advance of the attack.

We've been talking about the blizzard of information we deal with, but I think that if we talk to people in government they would talk about the blizzard of questions public officials have to answer. I finally appreciated this after many years of reporting when I got on the other side of the fence. You do begin to see things differently.

GREIDER: I wrote a piece, probably a lot like Dr. Barber's, back in August. It was less academic and more bilious about the president's bumbling, and it took issue with you all about why you weren't describing this reality.

Part of that piece was based on public record, but the biggest part of it resulted from just calling up my friends who cover the White House and asking, "How do you all feel about this?"

I was not surprised to learn that if you talk to reporters on that level they are happy to give you fresh, presumably accurate anecdotal evidence to confirm the portrait I drew.

It still seems to me that the White House press is not doing that kind of portraiture of this president. I'm not talking about picking at his word lapses. I'm on a more fundamental level. One of the answers, I thought, was that this White House devotes most of its energies to managing those images. Maybe "most" is an exaggeration, but they're very, very good at it, and they devote very serious attention to it every day.

ROWEN: I wonder if there is something less sinister than an organized attempt to protect the frailties or vulnerabilities of Ronald Reagan or any other president. I wonder whether we don't have something more generalized, because a lot of reporters have difficulty running through the typewriter what is running through their heads. There are a lot of fellows out there covering their beats and they know what's going on, but somehow they can't get the story down on paper or into the system.

Many an editor can go to reporters on the staff and dredge out stories that are simply not getting into the newspaper. I think what we may have here is an editing weakness as well as a reporting weakness.

RAINES: What I think happens at the White House is that the *Times* and the *Post* and some of the other institutions are committed to providing a stenographic record of the daily life of the presidency, simply reiterating what everybody else is saying that day.

If, instead, we were to turn our attention to really looking at the place and the process and the man and the people around him, I think we would have some success at fending off the kind of expert stage managing we see in this White House.

I'm not suggesting that you turn loose the random "Sojourner After Truth" to use that place as a pulpit. What I am suggesting is that if you sent a skilled reporter over there and said, "Let the AP carry the daily announcements and spend your time this week figuring out if there is any intellectual or policy communication between the president of the United States and the attorney general of the United States and what it is," you'd get an interesting story that I think would be a voyage of discovery. I don't think anyone over there right now can tell you what goes on between William French Smith and Ronald Reagan.

The other thing that I think is subversive of good reporting is the fascination with process and staff. "Jim Baker today advised Ronald Reagan to cut $30 billion from defense." Next day: "Ed Meese, in a powerful counter-offensive designed to reassert his primacy on the White House staff today told the president to add $30 billion to defense." This story goes on and on. It's a process story. By definition, a process story is going to be wrong part of the time and right part of the time. That's the sort of thing I wish we could get away from.

A final point on what Bill Greider had to say concerning the expertise of this White House in stage managing the presidency. Dave Gergen uses to an amazing degree the language of the theater. Ronald Reagan, in going about his job, uses the language of the theater. I will never forget my astonishment one day when he walked into the Oval Office, looked around at us and said, "Well, this is the right set. The lights are on."

There's great skill over there. Mike Deaver is a very skilled public relations professional who has spent something like 15 years crafting a public image of Ronald Reagan. I'm not addressing the question of whether it's a true image or a false image. I'm telling you it was built by a damn smart man, and it was built around a damn good performer. If you're going to try to break through the facade, you're not going to do it with the traditional daily chronological, stenographic kind of reporting.

The *Post* has three people at the White House. One is supposed to cover this daily grind. The others are free to pursue whatever. If they don't find it, if they're not able to translate it, it seems to me that's an affirmation of a point I made yesterday about our lack of insight and perhaps the incapacity of individuals involved.

Bart (Rowen) used a beautiful metaphor about running through the typewriter what you've got in your head, and I suggest that the problem with White House coverage, at least with some of our larger newspapers, is not that we tie up and shackle reporters through stenographic duties, but rather that we've been unable to shackle those who have the time and the motivation to do a better job, simply because they don't have the capacity to do it.

EVANS: I want to turn now to the White House and Ray Jenkins.

JENKINS: I have the uneasy feeling that I'm going to leave this conference as the man who's obsessed with rules. But I do want to say at the outset that since I am billed as speaking from inside government, which is more or less inside the bowels of the beast, I'm speaking as if I were still there rather than back doing honest work.

I'm interested in the metamorphosis of the title of the article in the *Atlantic*. It began with "The Education of David Stockman," period. Then the book adds "And Other Americans." I would like to make one more revision: "The Chief of Whom was William Greider."

What we're really talking about is the education of William Greider. George Orwell in his essay on "Why I Write," lists four reasons, and all of them are good. One is sheer egotism; another is aesthetic enthusiasm. One is historical purpose, leaving a record, and so on. And then there's one called political purpose. I think reporters have always been very uncomfortable with this.

Orwell means that you see the world as it should be and you try to achieve this by writing. We don't like that because that is in violation of the accepted myth of the journalist as a neutral observer who doesn't really influence events. On those rare occasions when we do influence events, and we can see the influence, it makes us very uncomfortable. That's why I think in Bill's fine introduction he was perplexed and disturbed. He stood back and said, "My God, what have I done?"

More particularly, he was disturbed at how the press had reacted to what he had done, and I think justly so, because the press did not concentrate so much on what he had reported as his method.

As I read his book, and throughout the conference here, I find myself coming back to several literary metaphors, all of which say the same thing. We've heard several times that we need to demythologize government. I'm going to take the position that we'd better be very careful because, however bad myths may be, they have served us, maybe not well, but they have served us.

Bill uses a metaphor in the book when he refers to the president as "the Wizard of Oz." I think all presidents are somewhat in the role of the Wizard of Oz, and in a sense Bill was Dorothy discovering the Wizard of Oz at the controls. Stockman happened to be the Wizard of Oz in this case. In fact Greider even says the same thing that Dorothy, disillusioned by what she's found, says to the Wizard of Oz, "Well, you're a very bad man." Do you remember his response? "No, I'm not a bad man. I'm just a very bad wizard."

GREIDER: I saw myself more as the Cowardly Lion.

JENKINS: Even after the discovery, both of them recognized that there were still things to be done. Dorothy had to get back, the Tin Man had to have whatever it was. And they still had to believe in this magic. The magic still had to work.

Even after the fraud was discovered, they went through the motions of making the magic work, and by going through the motions they made it work. So you have this curious blend of honesty and fraud as you did with Stockman who was saying one thing privately and another thing publicly.

Obviously you got Stockman in great trouble, and the reason you did is because that optimism is an absolute. It's the *sine qua non* of political success. It must be there, and what you did was expose Stockman's loss of optimism, if only momentarily. He was a flawed politician from that point forward. He still is.

The other metaphors are not all that original. The simplest is that you were the boy who cried out that the emperor had no clothes. Sitting around this table we say, yes, we knew all this was going on. We even knew that Stockman was thinking these things. But you were the one who blurted out, "He's naked."

It's very different to blurt out that David Stockman has no clothes than to say the government has no clothes. Bart had been doing that as early as February 1981, perhaps even earlier. That's not very sexy, but it is sexy when David Stockman is naked. The person who cries out that the emperor has no clothes better be prepared to get a rather sharp reaction.

All of these things are pretty well summed up in French novelist Jean Giraudoux's statement that there are truths which can kill a nation. I think that basically what he's saying is that we have to have some mythology. I know in the law, judges and lawyers have a device called legal fictions. They go back for centuries and what they mean is that in a terribly hard case for which there is no answer they'll contrive a fiction which becomes the foundation of the decision.

A very good example is the old common law fiction that when a man and a woman are married they become a single personality and that personality is spoken for by the man. Obviously that's a fiction on its face, but it has served for centuries. The law still is full of fictions of that kind. They serve until you find a better basis on which to make a decision or a public policy.

Obviously the other analogy, religion, is exactly the same. I can't even say what I regard as myth in religion without the possibility of offending someone around this table, but myth is absolutely essential. It's called faith instead of myth.

In government, I suppose the myth is one of order, of efficiency, a myth that things can be done. The press seems to be determined to destroy this myth although they recognize that it is a myth. We've said that it is. It's almost the theme of the Greider book. I doubt if anybody here realizes just how much damage Ronald Reagan has suffered because of this picture of chaos and confusion surrounding the budget process.

Someone on television yesterday morning used the phrase "confusion and disarray" in describing what was taking place. The *New York Times* used the term "outrageous" in describing the manner in which they were making these decisions. I have a feeling that these so-called backgrounders did not come from high levels, that they came from some lower level person. It might appear to him that there is chaos and confusion, but in fact this is the way things are done.

By creating an expectation of order and efficiency, and since this is the myth which sustains government, we have in effect inevitably set up the president for failure because if there's disorder, the president is incompetent. Maybe the rules need re-examination but if these rules didn't exist, new ones would have to be created. If the rules are bad, let's examine them and get rid of the ones that are bad. But we still have to live by certain rules of civility.

I know that you tended to cast aside my remark about breaking the photo opportunity rules, but it's fairly serious. It certainly was serious from the White House standpoint because it made a fool of the president. The press unilaterally changed the rules in that case.

W. E. (NED) CHILTON: Well, does the president need us more than we need him?

JENKINS: They're mutually dependent institutions, and any White House Press Office that gets at cross-purposes with the press will wind up with a new press secretary.

To me it seems that the picture is really a jigsaw puzzle, and we are jigsaw puzzle workers. We are supposed to take these odds and ends and pieces and fragments of information and put them together in a way that's coherent for the reader. I think, frankly, that we're failing at that.

I don't think we're failing because we're bad people. We're just bad wizards. And we usually fail for the same reasons government fails. People don't work hard enough. They cut corners when they ought not to cut corners. The answer is not to devise new forms of journalism. It's to re-examine the old ones, and ultimately it's going to depend on the quality of work we turn out. If we could just get all Bill Greiders and Steve Weismans and Howell Raineses for reporters, maybe everything would work out.

ZUCKERMAN: It seems to me to be implicit in what you're saying that the reality that underlies your mythology should be glossed over.

I am concerned about that because you say the reporters made a fool of the president, but I think the president made a fool of the president. If Bill Greider in his dialogue with David Stockman finds a way to illustrate this, it seems to me that is an enormous public service because that mythology which may be necessary to sustain a level of optimism in this country is going to run into a reality. That reality is called 11 or 12 percent unemployment and a collapsing economy over a period of time.

That may be a direct consequence of this policy if we don't somehow or other bring it to light. What is the role of the press? Is there no obligation on the part of the press to attack this mythology?

CARTER: Speaking from the government side, the government is not elected to do the job of the press. The government is not elected, the president is not elected, to do the job of his opposition. The president is not elected to bow to those whom he has defeated. The government is put in place to try to affect certain programs that are articulated in the campaign or brought up afterwards.

In that process the government will, and has a right to, attempt to manipulate the presentation of the news. It has a right and will attempt to shape the public perception of it, and it has a right to and will give or withhold facts as it sees best to affect its process.

Now, that is just a fact that—all the editorials, the sermons and the speeches and press gatherings aside—is what it should be doing. A problem arises when reporters and editors and columnists begin to believe that they ought to be participants in that process. One of the things that was most bothersome to me was not what Ray (Jenkins) sees as the problem—that is, the ravening mob—but it was watching the number of folks who really wanted to be players in our process.

There was a constant complaint to me that we didn't give enough information through our briefings. Any reporter who thinks he is going to get adequate, complete, and honest information from a government press briefing is a fool. And any reporter who begins and ends most of his reporting work with what official sources on background or up front say to him, is a fool and ought to be fired. The game is constitutionally, and I think morally, totally different.

Something Alexander Bickel said in the wake of "The Pentagon Papers" ought to be applied here. He said it is the presumed duty of government to govern, and of the press to publish, and the two should never confuse their roles.

It is absolutely a fact in Washington that too much of what passes for journalism is in fact participation in the process. To watch "Washington Week in Review" some weeks is to see people who truly believe that they are what their mythology makes them, the fourth branch of government.

The arrangements for covering government work well for the government, and work badly for the public. The system, as it has been perfected, makes the White House press essentially the captive of the White House; it makes the State Department press basically adjunct participants at State. The conventions of coverage are tailor-made to the manufacture of this blizzard of news with which we inundate you and with which we can control you.

EVANS: Is that deliberate?

CARTER: It's not deliberate. You are simply willing participants in what is to our benefit and not the public's. In the process you get no respect from us. For the most part those who are inside government look upon you with some contempt, a great deal of fear from time to time, but a running level of contempt. We feel about you the way Europeans feel about the Germans: You are either at our feet or at our throat, and you are to be treated like a dog, accordingly. We throw you the stuff we want to throw you to keep you at our feet. That consists in large part of trying to feed you at times which are appropriate to us but make you feel that you're being fed at times appropriate to you.

We think most of the time that you are useful in our communicating with audiences. You mostly serve as a useful conduit to one audience, the elites of Washington. You make possible a secondary form of communication between us. To a lesser degree you talk in our jargon to a public which frankly doesn't understand what it's reading because you're talking in terms that only make sense to the folks playing the game.

Too much of what you write on many of these beats is written for the approval of your fellow participants in the game, for your editors to some degree, and hardly at all for the comprehension and approval of a wider public, most of which you tend to think of with the same contempt as government officials. This public doesn't have the background to understand the stuff anyway, and you can't really write what you know because it would go over their heads.

I came to Washington extremely naive about government and in love with the press. I'm still in love with the press and in love with government itself. I'm less naive about both, and frankly I am disillusioned. That makes for easy cynicism about the way the press operates as opposed to the way it thinks it operates and the way it ought to operate.

But I cannot think of a single story with any real meaning in which there was not either a failure of emphasis or of fact. I'm not talking about the one-car accident story. I'm talking about the general run of stuff.

"That's your fault," says the reporter, "You lied to us." We can argue about that. You have to take it as a given that what you start with from the government is not what should be going out to the folks.

There's a great deal of laziness in the Washington press corps and we cultivate it. We cultivate it again by trying to make sure that there's a lot of stuff for you. We cultivate it with background briefings. We cultivate it by giving you information that you cannot use to hurt us, but that you do use to do good from our perspective. We so envelope you in the restrictions of form that when the information would be most useful to the public you can't use it. And when you do use it, it seems to be some kind of a surprise which causes a temporary fire storm, then it's gone.

You worry too much about words like "responsibility" and "credibility" and "institutional standing." And you worry too little about "vigor," and too little about the hard work of accurate reporting. You worry more, in fact, about whether you are going to have a difficult time getting to that Saturday night dinner party than you do about staying away from those dinner parties so you're clean enough to write the way you really see it.

The thing that overcame me most of all when I got to Washington was the discovery that the country club approach to journalism was, in fact, practiced regularly. I used to think that publishers and editors in one-paper small towns had a real problem with that kind of thing because they saw regularly the movers and the shakers at the country club and would carry their interpretation of events into their newsrooms.

Well, that's Washington. That just describes Washington on a regular basis. Dick (Harwood), you strain my faith in your credibility when you say that you don't really get close to the movers and shakers. Part of the game in Washington is to make sure a lot of you get close to us so that we can get you to put on the team jacket and then see to it that you don't take it off.

JENKINS: Who made that statement?

CARTER: John Chancellor said it of the State Department press corps under Henry Kissinger. And then he said, "What bothers me is they still haven't taken them off."

It is just a fact of much Washington coverage.

DAVIS: I'm going to just say three or four things about the way British economic coverage works. And there are three direct criticisms I wish to make, some of which I would also think are part of American coverage as well.

One is that the nature of the coverage leaves you in a state of complete ignorance about economics. The second is that there are two biases, quite subtle biases. One is a consistent pro-government bias which arises from the fact that reporters allow themselves to be manipulated by the government; and the second is a bias toward the center, a bias against the extremes, a bias against trade unions, a bias against most of the Labor Party, for example.

Yesterday Jim Carey asked for a protagonist press. Well, we have that in Britain, and it's appalling, because most of the newspapers use news simply as a way of boosting the party in power, the party they're supporting. You can see this on inflation coverage, for example. When inflation's coming down, most newspapers splash this on the front page because it's to Maggie's advantage. When inflation's going up, most newspapers will stick it on page seven.

There really isn't any economics in the newspapers. That leaves the vast majority of the people in Britain entirely uninformed, except from television, on the state of the economy.

I sat on a committee of inquiry into the mathematical ability of the British people a couple of years ago, and we decided to do an inquiry into how well the news was understood. Only about half understood the word "percentage." I suspect the same thing applies here. When you say, "Unemployment is down 27 percent this month," do you really know how many of your readers understand that term? Only 20 percent of the population could distinguish between rising prices and rising inflation. In other words, as long as prices were rising, they could not understand that inflation could be falling. They didn't understand the difference between "production" and "productivity." They didn't understand the difference between "nominal wages" and "living standards."

The thing that struck me yesterday was that the journalists sitting around this table have spent at least a tenth of their total news coverage this year and last year on the national budget. There's a massive number of budget stories in the papers. Yet we had two readers here yesterday. One of them said she wasn't interested in the budget. The other said it all went over his head. He couldn't understand any of it. The same is true in Britain. Even at the top end of the spectrum, there is massive use of jargon.

We've had a seminar here for two days. We've discussed very elitist questions of news coverage, whether it can be improved by depth and quality and all that sort of stuff. We've missed the basic issue, which to me is how you get ordinary people to understand the word inflation, how you get ordinary people to read any of the news you're writing on a subject you think is of vital importance, like the budget.

My second major criticism of the British press is that there is an underlying bias in favor of the government. It doesn't matter which government. I think this stems from the way they get their professional kudos. Professional kudos in Britain, and I suspect more so here, result from scoops, and most scoops in Britain involve publishing something the public is going to find out anyway in a couple of days.

The club system doesn't really work like this because it gives everybody the scoop at the same time. It is difficult, however, because it means that if the government chooses to single out someone who might have written a nasty story about the government, it can just exclude him from the club. Then he gets no more scoops.

The other thing about the pro-government bias, which I think must apply in all democratic systems, is what the government thinks is news. What the opposition thinks is much less likely to be news. Whatever the government thinks, because it thinks it, is news. If you take any paper and analyze the number of quotes from government, compared to the number of quotes from the opposition or from anywhere else you'll find there's a massive bias in favor of the government.

All those things give the government the benefit. In Britain it operates even better, because you have a thing called the Information Service, and as a newsman you're not supposed to approach anyone in government on the official level without going through the Information Service. Now, I sat in Number Ten five years working on economic policy at a reasonable level. I got one call from a press man in five years.

Finally, there's undoubtedly a solidly pro-right bias in the newspapers. I don't think anybody could deny that. There are some that are center-left, but there's a solidly pro-right bias. Then there is the question of what happens on television, where most people get access to most of their news. The BBC and ITV news teams are regarded as very impartial. And indeed, they count the number of mentions they give to the Labor politicians and Tory politicians and Social Democrats to make sure that the news coverage is fair.

However, I think that there's strong evidence now from people who have looked at the cumulative impact of the news over a long period of time, that news tends to support the common stereotype of the British economy. The common stereotype is that trade unions are at the root of all evil. They produce strikes. These strikes mean we have low growth in productivity; they mean that we can't sell goods in world markets, and they mean that we can't maintain our level of employment.

Now, this stereotype is even more clearly observed in foreign press coverage of Britain. It ignores, for example, that we lose half as many days in strikes per annum as you do per head of population. We sell twice the percentage of our national output on world markets. Our productivity growth is higher than yours. There is no mention of these things, either in our own media or in anybody else's because it doesn't fit the stereotype.

We've been doing many studies, some by the Glasgow Media Research Group, which show, for example, that British Leland, our major domestic car producer, loses more vehicles per year through management error, breakdowns and losses of supply, than it does in strikes—overwhelmingly more. Yet you never, ever see on the news that British Leland today lost 10,000 vehicles because of a management error. That isn't considered news. You only see British Leland today lost 10,000 vehicles because of trade union strikes.

One more example: There is an overwhelming bias in the UK press in favor of incomes policy, because trade union power and trade union dominance equals high wages which equals inflation. The Glasgow Group took a period of four months in 1975 and found 287 occasions where people favored wage controls and thought that the trade unions were for inflation. They found 17 occasions where the opposite point of view was argued.

So they found subtle bias toward the center, toward the stereotype of what makes the British economy tick. I think it's perpetuated on the news media.

EUGENE PATTERSON: What I wanted to say was that I was very much taken with both Hodding's and Gavyn's rather sobering examination of us from inside government. I'm not surprised. We know the government tries to tell less than the truth. We know, of course, that the press does not get at the truth, that we are constantly manipulated by government. And so we tend to be fairly cynical fellows.

I'm enormously impressed by the thesis that Ray Jenkins brought here. Because it takes me back again to the myths by which people live. We're more than just hooligan journalists. Maybe for a century the presidency could withstand much stronger scolding than we direct at it, but I would submit that the press was not nearly as powerful in those days as it is now.

Coming back to the basic idea of myths, I mentioned John Keegan's *Face of Battle* yesterday and the decision of the military officer-makers not to tell the full truth about the blast and the blood of battle, but instead to teach and drill in process, rationality, order, which then would stand up under the chaos of battle. Let's carry it further. Without the myth of a belief in God there would certainly be no faith in the better angels of our nature in this life, and no hope at the hour of our death. And without the myth of the lasting nature of romantic love, how much of an institution would marriage and the family amount to in this society?

It's a myth, no doubt, that there is order and efficiency in government. We know it's chaos inside, as you told us. But what, then, is the duty of the press? To expose that in a simple attack mode? We investigate and find the emperor wears no clothes. Do we find a further duty to society beyond that, to explain the incomprehensible, to go further than we already have, as simply roughnecks? Do we have a duty to society to try to explain things beyond explaining that the government is lying?

I guess what I've finally come down to is a belief that if man's myth—if man's mythic reach ceases to exceed his grasp—then have we, in fact, brought man face-to-face with reality? Or have we destroyed the true mythological reality by which man stumbles and cringes through this vale of tears?

The Nature of Public Understanding

OPENING STATEMENT BY:

Dr. John Robinson

SUMMATION BY:

W. E. (Ned) Chilton

HAROLD EVANS: I'm going to ask Dr. John Robinson, who's a psychologist, to tell us what he has learned about the nature of public perception and understanding, both in the United States and in the United Kingdom.

JOHN ROBINSON: We've referred already to the chaos in government. I'll talk a little bit about the chaos we find when we go out and talk to the public. I might mention that this has been something of a 20-year hobby of mine in terms of looking at the comprehension of various kinds of material.

If you get into the business of trying to inform the public, you're setting a role for yourself. I'm going to give you, I think, some glimpses into that. You've had a bit of it this morning in Gavyn's presentation of people's understanding of various concepts. But in large part it's a door that you might want to look through, rather than walk through. You should think carefully before proclaiming yourself interested in trying to get into this whole area.

I do think it is very important, and I'm going to describe some of the modest beginnings we've made in trying to monitor how one can follow trends in the comprehension of news stories.

The experience I had was working at the British Broadcasting Corporation for eight months in 1978. I had a lot of survey findings of the type that Gavyn had, which indicated very low public understanding of news events. I'd been bothered by this also, I suppose, because I had some particular notions about the way in which democracy ought to function.

I was also interested in seeing whether we could find some information that journalists, or some journalists, said they were interested in. They said, "We would really like to know what the public thinks. What does the public understand about these sorts of things?" So we worked for about eight months attempting to devise a methodology that would have credibility to television journalists. At the same time I sought to impose as little as possible the role of the social scientist in this whole process.

There are two techniques that we used on the project. One was the focus group where I would go to various parts of London just prior to the evening newscast, talk a bit about news in general, and then we'd watch the British Broadcasting Corporation newscast. Afterward we would have a discussion, followed by the ITV (Independent Television) broadcast, and some talk about differences between the two.

I would bring that information back to the newsroom the next day and give the editors and newsmen a chance to look at the reaction of people to their broadcast.

As a second technique, we tried with a representative sample to do large-scale studies in which we would use very open-ended questions to find out what people had picked up from particular news stories. I should say at the outset the early research I had done indicated very pessimistic results—less than 10 percent of what was on the average newscast was comprehended. The results that we came out with, I think, were much more optimistic on that particular score. There was 30 to 50 percent more in terms of basic comprehension of particular news stories.

One of the values of the technique we used is that we could get people to talk in their own words, and then try to code that information afterwards to see whether, in fact, the information seemed to be correct. In this particular case, I took the information from the news stories, the replies that people gave to each item in the newscast, and gave them to an editor saying, "Did these people get it right, or didn't they get it right, in terms of news?" That's where one gets this general sense of about 30 or 50 percent comprehension. But it was pretty depressing stuff for these men to look at because I think in large part they had a feeling there was 100 percent comprehension. You know, "We put it out there, we put it out very clearly, and these people just don't seem to get the story."

In large part, as I say, this was relatively depressing news to newsmen and the problem was trying to get a sense of how newsmen reacted to this particular kind of information. For the most part, I think they prefer to ignore it. It is a very difficult thing to come to grips with and to plan for.

Since we are dealing with economics another factor is built into understanding economic news. There were a couple of nights at the BBC when we were able to talk to people about some economic stories on the news and they said, "Well, those are figures. They say the inflation rate's gone up, but my wages haven't gone up. I haven't seen prices go up in this particular area. Those things are telling me what's going on already. Those really don't have any applications for me."

So there's a feeling that people are not able to understand because of structural reasons, but also the information isn't really useful because it doesn't apply to them and doesn't have any validity.

The second point on figures, which are very important for coverage of a lot of stories, is that there is a discount figure practically built into these stories. People generally tend to feel that politicians and government agencies use numbers for their particular purposes.

We decided to take a look at weekly news as more digestible pieces of information. We called up editors at BBC, ITV, the *Times* and the *Guardian* and asked them what were the major stories, what should the public have picked up this week in terms of the information provided. From that, we culled a list of eight questions that we then asked a cross section of the public.

The average correct score on that test was 2.3 of 8. There are various factors which lead to higher or lower scores. For example, those with more education scored 3.5 or 3.7, but people of less education were down to 1.5 or 1.6. That's about the range.

As a way of attempting to find out whether we were asking the right questions I decided to ask the same questions of BBC newsmen. Most of those I talked with said, "Oh, please don't ask me. I wasn't paying very close attention to the news story. I was off on special assignment."

But I pressed ahead anyway and said, "Well, I need some way to make sure that at least some of these questions are accurate." So I asked 10 BBC newsmen, and scoring them the same way we did the public audience, nine got all eight, and one got seven. There was not one person out of 507 British people who got a score higher than six. That indicates, I think, the tremendous gulf between the journalistic community in terms of the things you talk about and that you think are quite obvious, and what's going on, on a general level, with the public.

We're planning a replication study in the United States in the next year. We just tried out the instrument in the Washington area. We interviewed just 50 people, so these are not meant to be representative. But we came up with just about the same proportion of a 50 percent comprehension rate. We asked things like, what do people recall about developments in the Tylenol murder case? What happened to leaders of the Teamsters Union? What about the information on the attempted assassination of the Pope last year? President Reagan's newest proposal on the MX missile? What happened to the five-cent gasoline tax? Did they recognize Barney Clark, Caspar Weinberger and Yuri Andropov? Barney Clark beat Yuri Andropov, by the way, but most people described Barney Clark not as an artificial heart recipient, but as a heart transplant or a heart patient.

GERALD LANSON: Can you gauge whether in some cases it's a matter of people not being the news junkies we'd like them to be? In other words, are people not reading some stories so they are unfamiliar with them rather than not understanding them?

EVANS: It's either recognition or comprehension? Which is it?

ROBINSON: I don't know that we can tell. I think the point is that these are open-ended responses.

JAMES DAVID BARBER: What conclusion do you draw from the fact that those who identify Barney Clark correctly identified him either as a transplant or a heart case rather than as the recipient of an artificial heart?

ROBINSON: I'm not trying to say that they did not understand what's going on. What we would hope to do, at some later point would be to ask a more direct question.

W. E. (NED) CHILTON: Have you asked a question, say, on the tax issue which would hit them in the pocketbook, like the five-cent gas tax?

ROBINSON: About a quarter of the people we talked to said the tax had been tabled, which is what had happened to it. Another quarter said it had either been passed or failed. So 50 percent knew something about what was going on.

EVANS: What you're basically saying is that the results of this skirmish in Washington suggest that you're heading in the same direction as your much deeper research in Britain.

ROBINSON: In large part. One footnote, if I might, to all of these results. I saw a poll which had been done with regard to the David Stockman story. Almost 70 percent of those polled by NBC *News* had heard about the story that appeared in *Atlantic Monthly*. Seventy percent said that they had heard of that particular story, which I think is an indication that that was an extraordinary kind of event.

Interestingly, at the BBC, when we talked to people, we found that one of the greatest sources of information was news for the deaf. This is a program on BBC on Sunday evening for deaf people to recount exactly what happened during the week. The stories are done very slowly with captions across the bottom.

When you're talking about the British public, you have to realize that in terms of formal education, most journalists are college graduates or post graduates, while only about 20 or 25 percent of the general public has a comparable education. So there is a further difficulty in communicating with this audience. But even for that audience I think there is a need for more than good English or increased redundance. It's telling a story one way, and then coming back and weaving that particular element into several versions.

HODDING CARTER: That's a point that Bill (Greider) touched on and which I think is fairly commonly understood but isn't practiced. That is the necessity of saying in every story, this is the background and this is now what is happening and this is what the consequences are.

EVANS: I found complete resistance among editors when I was editing, to putting in a central background paragraph. They knew the background and they genuinely knew it, not just intellectually. They had so absorbed it into their bones that they felt the readers would get mad at them if they included it again. They were sure, there was no question that the readers knew it.

CARTER: People finally are beginning to realize that you do not have a permanent television audience. You have a floating audience. Some people watch one night and some people watch the next night and some people watch once a week.

Newspaper people like to think that their readership doesn't operate that way. But in fact you don't ordinarily read the whole paper every morning. This is a further argument for saying it over and over again.

WILLIAM GREIDER: I think what both of you have been saying is what I was trying to describe originally as a lack of context, which explains for me, at least, why the budget story didn't get through.

CARTER: But when you point out to me all that you wrote, I know I didn't read it every day because

I wasn't around. I'm a news junkie and I read everything.

EVANS: I'm a news junkie, too. In getting ready for this seminar, Don Baldwin went to enormous trouble to get a whole bunch of clips from a newspaper.

Going through those clips it was impossible for me to follow the news because I just didn't know what had happened when. Something had happened in between these developments, but they weren't spelled out. Any historical research on the daily press is a minefield of good information and a minefield of bewilderment and complexity.

It's as Jim Carey said. We assume the same reader reads the same paper at the same level of information. How can we get over this?

RAY JENKINS: I remember an experience I had when I was in Alabama. I felt that if there was any development in Southern politics I had a story in my back pocket that I could dictate to the *New York Times* right then and there.

Then they called me once and asked me to get an interview with John Sparkman, who had just become chairman of the Senate Foreign Relations Committee. Well, I got the interview, but I tell you that was the most terrifying experience of my life. I was utterly unprepared to question one of my own constituents, and here I was an editor. I was so unprepared about foreign affairs that I couldn't even conduct a simple interview.

EUGENE PATTERSON: It seems that much of what we have said here is an extension and ratification of the point Bill Greider made in his book, that we are telling too many stories in daily slices incomprehensible to the average reader. Second, the example of his Stockman piece in *Atlantic* does not go to yesterday's discussion of the media being the message. This is a magazine story which a newspaper can't do.

It seems to me we need to re-examine newspaper journalism to the extent that we could do what we used to call a lean back story. When you're so deep into a budget story slice by slice, day by day, you should do a Greider lean back, give it a few pages of newsprint and tell a gripping narrative in ways that people will read.

HOWELL RAINES: On one of the daily slices, how important do you think it is that element X is in the third paragraph or the ninth paragraph? Is the inverted pyramid structure too deeply imbedded in our brains?

PATTERSON: I think that we have to experiment with writing techniques. If we go all the way to the anecdotal lead-in, then you get the *Wall Street Journal* mindset which I find maddening on some mornings. I want to read those three stories on page one, but I haven't got time, so I go way down looking for the nut graph and then try to find out what this guy is getting at.

RAINES: The way to make an economic story or any complex issue comprehensible is to write it in a narrative chain that the reader can follow. I've had this conflict with myself many times. If a point is important, I've got to move it to the top rather than just structuring the facts so they carry the reader on an orderly march.

PATTERSON: I really believe, though, going back to my wire service days in the *United Press,* that whether you're writing a plane crash or a budget story you can best serve the reader by giving him a catch-all lead. Hugh Bailey used to say no *United Press* lead should get on the wire unless it makes the reader say, "Oh, my God!"

GREIDER: I think the point several people have made is that the word narrative has a whole collection of implications that are in conflict with the way news is generally organized.

Newspapers, and not just newspapers, but television, are suspicious of that form because they see it as a form of fiction. My argument would be that all forms are a form of fiction, and that there's reality and realism in narrative.

JAMES CAREY: All the examples we have used here involve a dramatic structure. Most styles of reporting are almost destined to keep people at a distance rather than getting them involved. If we stop talking about involving people on a large scale as opposed to relatively small audiences, you're not going to do without some dramatic structure. People tend to remember that which they talk about. If it doesn't have a compelling quality, if it doesn't lead them to remember and to talk about it with others, you're not going to get very good comprehension scores.

ROBINSON: Now, in regard to a couple of other things which we picked up from our BBC study which I think dovetail with other research.

One is that you cannot be explicit enough in communication. Leaving something between the lines and thinking the reader is going to get it is a very dangerous practice.

I see the research we did there as really having minimal impact because of the depressing nature of the results. I really don't know a way around this. And the question is, what are the incentives for a journalist to produce a more comprehensive product?

I've had running debates with people in which I've said, if you want to increase comprehension of the news, I think I could probably increase it 25 or 30 percent. But I don't know whether you're going to get more of an audience, whether reporters are going to be any happier in the job or whether you're going to retain any of your best reporting talent as a result. I'm not really sure, when you look at the incentives of the cost and the benefits, whether it's something you want to get into.

PATTERSON: You've got to believe it is.

ROBINSON: I'd like to believe it is, but I'm not sure.

PATTERSON: I don't have full figures to back me up, but I bet you I can get them. Our newspaper hired a longtime foreign correspondent who was the UPI foreign editor as our one-man foreign service.

We send him off four or five times a year to Russia or the Middle East or Japan or wherever the story is and in between he writes little essays that we anchor on page two.

The kind of correspondence he does is a "letter home" from a correspondent and our readers have gotten to know him. I would guess that he is second only to our sports editor as the best read personality in our newspaper. This is international news, which is supposed to have zero readership in provincial newspapers. He's brought it alive, simply by making it a human interest story.

ROBINSON: There is also a less honorable side to all of this, which you may have seen in terms of the process of news and research. That is the news doctors who across the country are doing quite well in terms of changing the face of American television news. I'm not sure they have increased the share in market, but they've increased audiences. They have been profitable. I suspect they have increased comprehension levels, but levels of journalism probably suffer as a result.

LANSON: First of all, John mentioned that the "why factor" is something that helps readers understand. I think any good reporter should say why it is and should say it high in the story.

The problem I have is, I don't think that in daily journalism the answer is always obvious. And I think that if the press makes an effort to concentrate on informing readers, the result may be that we'll misinform readers if the "why" is incomplete.

I think that basically this is where I disagree with Bill Greider. I don't disagree with the need to look back over a period of time to do what Gene calls lean back stories, which I think are very useful.

I also think that on a daily basis, we can provide better contexts and that the press has the right and responsibility to ask questions if the questions aren't being asked or answered. It's acceptable for us to ask those questions and I think gaps sometimes develop because the newspaper is focusing on one particular segment of a story rather than the full story.

Just to reiterate what's been said many, many times, I think the press needs to try harder to make the business of government public. There is some eagerness to be an insider, and the ground rules give a reporter the sense that I know what's going on, you know what's going on, we can talk about it in the bar and we'll agree to let this much get out to the public.

I also think that something Dick Harwood said the *Washington Post* does is very good. On truly major stories editors should consider assigning backup teams, reporters who are unencumbered by the demands of daily stories, people who would have a better overview and who could lay out in documentary fashion the chaos of a period of weeks or months. Reporters should be reminded, and perhaps editors as well, about the wealth and range of sources, both print and people sources, available to them.

Many newspapers would benefit from a first-rate documents course. I don't see too much of the I. F. Stone reporting in Washington today. I see a lot more people talking to sources inside the government. It doesn't do much for me to pick up yesterday's *Times* and find out that somebody in the administration is considering a freeze on the budget. It's the lead story in the *Times*. I can read it but I still can't comprehend it because there is no name attached. It's basically useless to me.

EVANS: For what it's worth may I say that I see very little of what I call action analysis in which names and attitudes and anecdotes are included with the analysis.

The analysis can be written in journalistic form, but this journalistic form, if you'll forgive me, seems to be very rare in the United States. In fact, your pages are generally structured not to have it.

Something which is a schism between the two may come in your new perspective section or a section of the *New York Times,* but generally it seems to be against the canons and ethics of American journalism. It's something that we did every week in London, although sometimes very imperfectly.

HOBART ROWEN: May I say something more or less responsive to what Gerald Lanson was saying. I think in general that what we just heard is too harsh as a total judgment. It's too harsh on us. I agree that we should use analysis stories at the top of the page, if it's the best story of the day. There's a prejudice in the *Washington Post,* almost a fixed rule, against using an analysis story, either as a lead or off-lead. I think there's no reason for that.

I also agree that obviously we need to get away from the canned briefing, develop our own sources and declare our independence of spoonfeeding by the government. But I don't see this business as a sort of a conscious cabal between the government press agent and the reporter in Washington with everybody conspiring to keep the tidbits to titillate cocktail parties rather than publishing them in the paper.

I don't really believe that happens, however clubby some of the atmosphere may be. I don't think that is the way good reporting is done in Washington. I don't think you're giving a number of good reporters enough credit for getting some pretty good stories and doing it independently. Finally, I really do think that when you make such a fixed rule on non-attribution you can say that you're really thinking it through. You've got to make some assumptions. You've got to give some credibility to the source, the sense of the paper you're dealing with.

Now, presumably at some point down the road we're going to get more. But you're not saying, are you, that the reader should be denied the knowledge that one of the things being discussed now at a reasonably high policy level in Washington is a freeze? I think that would be crazy, denying the public something that's essential.

LANSON: An unnamed source for a budget story says a freeze is being considered. Very often when the press reports things like this someone in the administration is floating a trial balloon. Somebody is attempting to manipulate. The story goes like this, the public doesn't read it every day and the public gets lost.

CARTER: Worse than that. The fact is, the lead story or second lead story in the *New York Times* for several days this last week consisted of stories like this from anonymous sources. There will be a $25 billion cutback on the domestic side. No, there won't. There's going to be an up on defense or a down on defense. No, there won't. Up it goes, down it goes, all anonymous.

Do you think public comprehension and understanding emerges from that kind of exercise? This kind of stuff is useful to the reporter who gets a good story. It's useful to the guy floating it because he gets a chance to see whether the thing will get off the ground. It isn't useful to the public, which simply doesn't understand what is happening.

EVANS: In terms of public understanding, you could carry a story in the *New York Times* saying nobody in the government would give us a statement on-the-record of what was going on about the budget.

CARTER: I think anybody could sit down and improve the way the story was written. I was talking to a narrow point. Do you say that we're going to give the reader no information because we cannot at this point provide a complete story?

Do you say to the reader, "Dear reader, we could tell you some undefined, unattributed source says there's going to be a freeze, but other people won't say it, so therefore we're not going to tell you the rest."

RAINES: I hear in some of Hodding's words the voice of Jody Powell, which would reduce us to an informational paralysis if we took too seriously this kind of indication about error A or miscalculation C.

So I agree with Bart Rowen there is utility in the public knowing what ideas are being discussed. Just because the budget freeze is not yet a reality doesn't mean that the poor taxpayers don't have a right to know that they're talking about it.

CARTER: My point is that the least you can do in a story like this is to identify what section of the White House it comes from. Does this come from those who are classically understood to be big defense spenders? If so, it represents something substantive. Or does it represent the fifteenth wave from the same faction which has always been asking for something along these lines?

LANSON: To sum up what I'm saying, I think if you rely on this kind of source, you rely on catch phrases. This is not because you can't get the information. It's buzz reporting and a certain amount of laziness. When you get away with doing that, day in and day out, you don't have to push to get your sources.

ROWEN: There may be a laziness factor, but it's easier to sit here and say you've got to get out and push more and get more, compared to getting it in time and getting it in the paper. There's a difference between theory and reality and a lot of people I know push as hard as they can.

EVANS: I think over the two days we have reflected the importance of reporting, but I think it would be wrong to leave the impression that news is something you go and get from a named or unnamed government source.

News is very often out there, waiting to be reported. It's what's happening to small business, it's what's happening to unemployed blacks. Let's not leave the impression with readers that we think that the government has a cupboard full of news with and without names.

Bill Greider, I'm going to give you a chance to claim victory or a draw, whatever it is.

GREIDER: I was struck, and I think a little surprised, at the unanimity on the question of whether the news gets through, and when we argued about techniques nobody stood his ground and said, hey, it works. In two days, nobody argued that it works. I had thought this would be a major point of contention.

When I have tried to wheedle wisdom from Professor Barber, he would never tell me anything, but he would ask a question. And the question he would always ask is, "Compared to what?" This is not a bad question for reporters to hear now and again.

We don't know "compared to what" in this situation, because nobody did research like John Robinson in the 1920s or the 1890s. We don't know whether the curve is up or down. My reading of history tells me it's up, and that however abysmal comprehension levels are at this point, or however crude newspapers and everything else are in communicating, they're probably somewhat better than they were two generations ago or 100 years ago.

I think there's a price for that. I would argue that if you believe the curve is up, then this is not a static point in history or a new dilemma for democracy.

Now I take one more step back to report a conversation Dick Stout and I had last night about what happens to mass media organizations. It's not hard to imagine a future 10 to 20 years from now when all of our arguments of these past days would sound precious and irrelevant to the economic marketplace.

EVANS: You mean newspapers are going to disappear or change?

GREIDER: No, I'm talking about the corporate conglomeration of newspapers and all of these wonderful intriguing new formats and different voices and so forth we want to see flourish in newspapers. I could as easily predict a future in which Gannett owns the world and Gannett has absolutely no interest in doing any of these things.

CHILTON: How can you not predict that future?

GREIDER: Well, I'm not going to argue it here. I think it's too late to open that door. I'm just suggesting that there's nothing in the present economic landscape of newspapers that would suggest that everybody is going to pick up the transcript of this meeting and try to apply it to their newspapers, with a few notable exceptions.

EVANS: Now to Ned Chilton for a summing up.

CHILTON: It's too bad all of us can't have a last say to list the highlights of this splendid meeting. To me it's tentative; it was taken down at the time; it's capsuled. And while I regard these as the highlights, I'm sure everybody else would have a different opinion.

Greider talked of the press-government symbiosis, of what's going to happen about concentrating on the question of what did happen. Is the news media responsible to its readers? What are their failings, what are our failings?

Harwood came back and said the press is not insiders but outsiders. And we can't communicate the reality of many international tangles because the sad truth is we don't know those realities.

We mustn't delude ourselves about our capabilities. "We are skillful hacks faced with duties we can't perform." Then he asked, do we underestimate our readers?

I have an aside here. Do you all remember those lists of the top 10 or 20 stories of the year, compiled by editors? Well, go out and ask the public what are the 10 or 20 top stories of the year. Then look at the differences.

Information moves quicker than ever, ideas slower than ever. Is there truth out there to be gotten? Patterson said the press is giving the public a false idea of the coherence and effectiveness of government. What does the press owe its government? Is the press getting across enough of the blood and guts of government?

Then Dave Barber asked, "How is the press being received by the public?" We don't know.

Barber also said we overestimate reality and underestimate illusion.

Harwood said the mythology of what a newspaper is and what a newspaper does was capsulated by his statement that each day the *Post* prints more comics than it does national news.

Last, journalists don't trust the governed, why should the governed trust journalists? That's an excellent point.

Lansner then gave us a resume on polling, and pointed out that by an 8-to-1 margin, people wanted cuts in federal government. Yet historically, in poll after poll, 55 percent favor wage and price controls.

He said the public is skeptical of simultaneous budget and tax cuts. But after extensive campaigns to sell the American people on Reaganomics, most Americans favored same.

Barber said newspapers should listen to academicians on the business of polling, but he really didn't tell us what we should do with the polls.

Davis reported on a poll in Britain—and I found this fascinating. The question was, when will the rate of inflation hit 5 percent, and it was about to hit 5 percent. One percent of the populace gave the correct answer.

Our leader then asked, "If you take the personality out of journalism, what do you have?" A lot of facts, that's what you have.

Mr. Zuckerman spoke of the international debt mess, and I found this fascinating. Speaking of the possible collapse of the western banking system, he asked, "Should papers tell the whole story and risk a run on banks?" That comes back to the question, it seems to me, that Patterson asked earlier: "What do papers owe their international bankers?"

Raines said public officials try to use reporters, and reporters try to use public officials. Is it fair to quote a president verbatim when he spouts nonsense? Older reporters are patriotic optimists, younger reporters bend over backwards to be fair to presidents. In other words, presidents always win.

Raines ended his talk with a *mea culpa:* the longer he stays in Washington, the more comfortable he gets. He also advocated more new reporters in Washington and beat rotation. I thoroughly agree with that.

Harwood says there's an institutional interest in what a reporter asks, and that one man's outrage is another man's political gain.

Rowen said one problem with coverage of the big story is the inability of reporters to get down on paper what is in their heads.

Jenkins said presidents aren't bad men, just bad presidents. I agree with that, and I also believe that if we're a government of the people, which we profess to be, it's essential that the people learn that their leaders aren't Thors or Zeuses. Who else is to do this job than the press? No one else is.

Hodding Carter said the president has the right to manipulate the press, but the press shouldn't voluntarily be a party to manipulation. The press too often forgets for whom the press is providing news, and the press often takes as a given that the governors well may be speaking with a forked tongue.

Davis said the nature of the coverage of economic news was not understandable. Britain has a partisan press, mainly conservative. People don't understand economics. Remember what Winston Churchill said? He said he did not understand economics or economic theory, but he thought shooting the head of the Bank of England was a pretty good idea.

Davis said further that there's an underlying bias in favor of government by the press of Great Britain. I'm wondering—and this is an aside—mightn't Davis's accusation also apply to the American press?

Carter then said, "You think we lie to you and when you learn we haven't, you think we tell you the truth." That's a stunning observation and I mean that. I've heard it before, but I'm glad I was reminded of it.

Patterson said we have a duty to explain the incomprehensible after bringing the incomprehensible to the attention of our readers.

Robinson said there's a huge gulf between news personnel's understanding of a story and the public's perception of the same story and he said repetition and background are important.

That ends my report.

EVANS: Thank you very much, Ned. That's an excellent report and I don't need to say any more, except to thank everybody who's been here. I want to thank Modern Media Institute for putting this on and you all for providing what I thought was a fascinating and rewarding session.